Unlocking Mathematics Teaching

Now in a fully updated second edition, *Unlocking Mathematics Teaching* is a comprehensive guide to teaching mathematics in the primary school. Combining theory and practice, selected experts outline the current context of mathematics education. They suggest strategies, activities and examples to help develop readers' understanding and confidence in delivering the curriculum. The book combines an accessible blend of subject knowledge and pedagogy, and its key features include:

- advice on teaching mathematics to high and low attainers;
- guidance on teaching mental maths;
- ideas for incorporating ICT;
- guidance on assessment in mathematics education;
- teaching problem solving;
- numerical and non-numerical examples;
- updated references, taking into account the Williams Report.

This book will be of interest to all primary education students and practising teachers looking to increase their confidence and effectiveness in delivering the mathematics curriculum.

Valsa Koshy is Professor of Education at Brunel University. Her main areas of work are mathematics and education and the professional development of teachers.

Jean Murray is Professor of Education at the University of East London.

Unlocking Mathematics Teaching

Second edition

Edited by Valsa Koshy and Jean Murray

Routledge
Taylor & Francis Group

LONDON AND NEW YORK

First edition published 2002 as *Unlocking Numeracy*
by David Fulton Publishers

This edition published 2011
by Routledge
2 Park Square, Milton Park, Abingdon, Oxon, OX14 4RN

Simultaneously published in the USA and Canada
by Routledge
711 Third Avenue, New York, NY 10017

Routledge is an imprint of the Taylor & Francis Group, an informa business

British Library Cataloguing in Publication Data
A catalogue record for this book is available from the British Library

Library of Congress Cataloging-in-Publication Data
Unlocking mathematics teaching/edited by Valsa Koshy and Jean Murray. – 2nd ed.
p. cm.
Originally published: Unlocking numeracy/edited by Valsa Koshy and Jean Murray. 1st ed,
Includes index.
1. Numeracy–Study and teaching (Primary) 2. Mathematics–Study and teaching (Primary) I. Koshy, Valsa, 1945– II. Murray, Jean, 1955– III. Unlocking numeracy.
QA135.6.U55 2011
372.7–dc22
2010040716

ISBN13: 978-0-415-57929-2 (hbk)
ISBN13: 978-0-415-57928-5 (pbk)
ISBN13: 978-0-203-82846-5 (ebk)

Typeset in Bembo by Prepress Projects Ltd, Perth, UK
Printed and bound in Great Britain by TJ International Ltd, Padstow, Cornwall

Contents

Illustrations

Tables

Boxes

Notes on contributors

Ron Casey is Senior Research Fellow of the Brunel Able Children's Education (BACE) Centre at Brunel University. Research and development projects he is currently involved with include devising models for mathematical provision for able mathematicians and writing materials for mathematics enrichment for primary school pupils. He has written a number of publications to support teachers in teaching mathematically gifted pupils. His subject expertise is in mathematics and science. Ron has a special interest in the role of creativity in mathematics and the development of mathematical processes in children.

Caroline Clissold is an experienced primary school teacher, having taught all ages from Years 1 to 6. For nine years, she was the mathematics consultant for Richmond upon Thames, implementing the National Numeracy Strategy, and subsequently the renewed version, into the borough. She now works as a freelance consultant and her current work includes regional coordinator for the NCETM, delivering INSET for BEAM, supporting teaching and learning in various local authorities in London and part-time lecturer at Brunel University. She has had many articles and books published. Her main interest lies in developing ways to link objectives to each other and the wider curriculum, and integrating using and applying and speaking and listening skills in a meaningful and engaging way.

Rachel Fairclough has taught mathematics within several 11–18 comprehensive schools based in Essex, Oxfordshire, Surrey and Slough. She worked for two years in a private school in Richmond where she was head of faculty (science, mathematics and ICT). In addition to her work as a Key Stage 3 numeracy consultant for a variety of local education authorities she worked for Brunel University as a course tutor in mathematics in the School of Education. She has been able to expand her university work with secondary postgraduate initial teacher training into her present role teaching mathematics in school. She is currently involved in writing materials for and delivering a 'raising achievement through enrichment' project, coordinated and based at Brunel University.

John Garvey is Senior Lecturer in Education at St Mary's University College with responsibility for mathematics and ICT. Prior to his career in higher education, he was a primary school teacher for seven years and the head teacher of a primary school in the London Borough of Richmond upon Thames. He has particular research interests in data handling and the use of interactive whiteboards for learning and teaching.

Mark Humble taught mathematics in secondary schools for thirteen years, holding a number of posts including head of department and advisory teacher for mathematics with a London local education authority. Moving into higher education, he became the Head of Mathematics in the School of Education at Brunel University. In 2005 Mark moved to Kingston University to undertake a similar role and to teach on both primary and secondary teacher education courses. He has also undertaken extensive consultancy work in mathematics for local education authorities. Mark's research interests include the processes of mathematical problem solving and numeracy development in the later years of schooling.

Sarah Jackson-Stevens is Senior Lecturer in Primary Mathematics at Kingston University. After a degree in music, specialising in piano and violin, she qualified as a primary teacher at Kingston University. Having taught in primary schools in Somerset she returned to London in 2002 to work in higher education. Sarah is interested in the links between music and mathematics – particularly the notion of self-efficacy beliefs in music performance and whether these attributes may be transferred in any way when supporting students' mathematical development as they prepare for primary teaching. Her research interests include assessment and the role of motivation in the learning process. In her spare time Sarah is a qualified advanced personal trainer, is learning to play golf and continues to indulge her passion for music

Bob Jeffery is a freelance educational consultant and a former senior lecturer at Brunel University. He is a former chair of the Association of Teachers of Mathematics and has wide experience in teacher education. He has been course leader for an innovative Master's degree in Primary Mathematics and English and led several large European teams working on the reform of education systems in Poland and Lithuania.

Valsa Koshy is Professor of Education at Brunel University. Before joining the university she was an advisory teacher for mathematics. She has taught initial training students and had responsibility for mathematics professional development programmes for a number of years. She has led several government-funded mathematics projects, supporting teachers with both subject and pedagogical knowledge. At present she leads several action research projects with teachers from several local authorities on enriching mathematical learning of children aged from 4 to 11 years. Her particular interests are mathematics education, educating higher ability students, assessment and action research for professional development of teachers. She has written several books, many of which are in mathematics education.

Jean Murray taught in Inner London primary schools for nine years before moving into higher education to teach mathematics to intending teachers at the School of Education, Brunel University. In 2007 she became Professor of Education and Research Leader in the Sir John Cass School of Education at the University of East

London, where she maintains a keen interest in researching children's learning patterns in mathematics. Jean has undertaken extensive national and international consultancies in mathematics for schools, education authorities and national organisations such as the British Council, the Department for Education and the National Numeracy Strategy.

Debbie Robinson has worked in education for over thirty years: as a classroom teacher in both secondary and primary schools, an advisory teacher and a training consultant planning and delivering teachers' courses for BEAM and Education Authorities as well as a teacher trainer initially at Brunel University. Her work has involved research on the Graded Assessment in Mathematics Project at King's College and the TVEI and Mathematics Project at the Institute of Education. She has co-written the book *Teaching Mental Strategies* as part of her consultancy work for BEAM and contributed a chapter to *Unlocking Creativity: A Teacher's Guide to Creativity across the Curriculum*. She is currently teaching mathematics on both the undergraduate, postgraduate and Master's courses at St Mary's University College, where she continues to research the development of creative approaches to teaching through the use of resources.

Acknowledgements

We would like to thank the many children, student teachers and teachers we have worked with and learnt from over the years. This book represents the collective endeavours of the contributors who have worked with children and both initial training and practising teachers. We would also like to express our gratitude to our past colleagues, Jan Potworoski and Christine Mitchell, for the support and inspiration they gave us during our work at Brunel University.

Introduction

Valsa Koshy and Jean Murray

Mathematics education in schools in England is at a critical point. A decade ago, the National Numeracy Strategy (NNS) (DfEE 1999) was introduced by the British government; this later became part of what was referred to as the National Primary Strategy. The purpose of the NNS was to help schools and practising teachers to raise children's achievement in mathematics. The strategy team has been offering a range of support to schools – in terms of both professional development courses and materials. In March 2011, the NNS will come to an end, although we hope that the expertise developed by practitioners through this initiative will continue to have some influence on the quality of learning and teaching mathematics. Among new developments in mathematics education there have been two important milestones. First, Professor Adrian Smith (DfES 2004) conducted a ground-breaking enquiry into mathematics education, which made recommendations for raising the status of mathematics in the curriculum through effective professional development of teachers and by increasing the supply of mathematics graduates into the profession. The government pledged to take action to raise our young people's interest in mathematics and to improve the quality of teaching and learning of mathematics. Following the Smith Report, the influential Williams Review (Williams 2008) into primary mathematics teaching renewed the message that, irrespective of the age and stage of a child, a high-quality curriculum and excellent teaching are two conditions for successful learning of mathematics. As the report explains, the National Curriculum for England and Wales (DfEE/QCA 1999) sets out the decisions that determine the knowledge, skills and understanding deemed to be essential for all children. It is stressed that, no matter how good the curriculum, it cannot benefit children in the absence of excellent teaching.

There is a shortage of published research into mathematics education in the UK. However, based on a review of international research in both primary and secondary mathematics education, Slavin (2009) emphasises that it is effective teaching strategies and not the curriculum which can make a real difference to the quality of teaching. Slavin goes on to say that 'Changing the way children work together, and classroom management and motivation, can improve the maths outcomes for all pupils' (Slavin 2009: 3).

How do we enhance the quality of mathematics teaching? Many years of working with teachers and teacher trainees have led us to believe that the teacher has a central role in enlightening children about the beauty of mathematics. We hope that mathematics teaching is an event in which you, the readers of this book, will participate in the many years to come. This book is offered as the key to unlocking the door of opportunity, enabling you to engage in that participation. The words of an eminent mathematician should provide the beacon inspiring you to participate in your endeavour with dedication. Hardy (2007) first wrote in 1940 that

> A mathematician, like a painter or a poet, is a maker of patterns. If his patterns are more permanent than theirs, it is because they are made of ideas (p. 84)

and

> The mathematician's patterns, like the painter's or the poet's must be beautiful; the ideas, like the colours or the words, must fit together in a harmonious way. (p. 85)

School inspection reports on mathematics teaching (Ofsted 2008) highlight the importance of the teacher's role and enthusiasm in developing positive attitudes in children towards mathematics. During school visits the inspectors found that children had a narrow view of the nature of much of mathematics teaching and they highlight what difference a teacher's enthusiasm can make. Ofsted found that too often pupils were expected to remember methods, rules and facts without grasping the underpinning concepts, making connections with earlier learning and other topics and making sense of the mathematics so that they can use it independently. A model of teaching with predetermined answers to routine work may stifle originality and creativity. The excessive focus on the acquisition of facts and skills and solution of routine exercises can contribute to mathematical anxiety. In these circumstances, how do we encourage children to appreciate the beauty of mathematics that Hardy refers to and encourage them to want to learn the subject? One of the ways to achieve this is to encourage children to develop what Johnston-Wilder and Lee (2010) refer to as *mathematical resilience*, which they believe is more difficult to build in mathematics. The authors explain: 'mathematical resilience is about understanding, but it is also about building confidence in that understanding and about being in a position to learn mathematics that is as yet, unknown' (p. 38).

To become effective teachers of mathematics we also need to consider the objectives of teaching mathematics. The specific objectives set out in the National Numeracy Strategy are a good starting point and will continue to influence mathematics teaching. These objectives are to:

- have a sense of the size of a number and where it fits into the number system;
- know by heart number facts such as number bonds, multiplication tables, doubles and halves;
- use what they know by heart to figure out answers mentally;
- calculate accurately and efficiently, both mentally and with pencil and paper, drawing on a range of calculation strategies;

- recognise when it is appropriate to use a calculator, and be able to do so effectively;
- make sense of number problems, including non-routine problems, and recognise the operations needed to solve them;
- explain their methods and reasoning using correct mathematical terms;
- judge whether their answers are reasonable and have strategies for checking them where necessary;
- suggest suitable units of measuring, and make sensible estimates of measurements;
- explain and make predictions from the numbers in graphs, diagrams, charts and tables.

In addition to the above list of objectives, in this book we have also specifically focused on the following aspects:

- how to improve the quality of teaching by considering aspects of pedagogy, such as problem solving, use of ICT and assessment of learning;
- giving a high profile to using and applying mathematics;
- how to meet the specific needs of groups of children – both low attainers and the more able;
- providing practical ideas for teaching mathematics that have been found to work in classrooms;
- exploration of different mathematical ideas and terminology to enhance the readers' understanding of issues.

We hope that the contents of this book will support teachers and those who are training to teach to reflect on aspects of teaching, so as to enhance the quality of teaching. One of the aims of this book is to offer teachers opportunities to reflect on issues and promote debate. A balance of theory, reference to recent research and practical strategies is offered with the intention of supporting teachers to improve classroom practice.

The chapters in this book have been informed by the three interacting roles of the contributors: their many years of experience of providing mathematics professional development courses to hundreds of teachers, involvement in initial training of teachers and their own research into aspects of mathematics education. Some of the ideas introduced here are new and have not have been dealt with in other publications.

In Chapter 1, Bob Jeffery invites the reader to experience numeracy by trying out some tasks. He introduces aspects of teaching numeracy by explaining the underlying principles according to which we should teach numeracy. By carrying out the tasks, the reader will not only develop a robust understanding of concepts, but also appreciate the implications of teaching these concepts to children. The ideas developed in this chapter have been used as a basis of much of the mathematics teams' teaching of the in-service and initial training courses.

In Chapter 2, Caroline Clissold and Mark Humble explore the importance of giving children opportunities to apply and use their mathematical knowledge and understanding through an appropriate range of problem-solving and investigative activities. They argue that knowledge and understanding of the facts, skills, concepts and strategies of mathematics (the knowledge base of mathematics) and the skills of mathematical thinking can be simultaneously developed and enriched through the use of appropriate learning contexts. Their chapter offers examples of how three broad types of activities – an extended number activity, integrating mathematics into other curriculum subjects and a mathematical investigation – can be used as contexts for developing both mathematical thinking and knowledge in Key Stage 2. Between them these three types of activities aim to offer children opportunities to develop and enrich their awareness of the world of mathematics. The examples show how working within mathematics as a subject and across other subjects of the school curriculum, notably art, literacy and geography, can provide creative learning and teaching contexts.

In Chapter 3, Debbie Robinson considers some important issues relating to teaching mental mathematics. She draws on her own practice in teaching mathematics and knowledge of how children learn and understand ideas, as well as her experiences of working with both initial training and practising teachers. She focuses on two key questions: 'What is mental calculation?' and 'How can we enable children to develop effective strategies for mental calculation?' She facilitates analysis and reflection on these questions. Debbie places the teaching of mental mathematics within the main objectives for teaching mathematics and discusses elements of teaching styles and organisation that should enhance the effectiveness of classroom provision.

In Chapter 4, John Garvey highlights the value of ICT in investigating real-life contexts that will get children talking about mathematical ideas. His chapter identifies how teachers with a keen understanding of the potential of ICT have provided children with contexts in which they can develop skills of representing, organising and interpreting information with a view to deepening their understanding of the world around them. The ICT applications described include the use of programmable robots and the program 'Counting Pictures' in Key Stage 1 and the use of branching databases and spreadsheets in Key Stage 2. Central to the teaching and learning contexts John describes are strategies such as the appropriate use of open-ended and closed questions, the focus on children talking through mathematical ideas, the planning of practical mathematical activities embedded within tasks involving the use of ICT and the conscious encouragement of different modes of representing information.

In Chapter 5, Rachel Fairclough provides illuminating ideas on problem solving in mathematics and how these can be developed in children. Although problem solving is part of the numeracy strategy and is included in all national initiatives, this topic has not received the attention it deserves. The author provides a framework for analysing different types of problems and invites the reader to consider what processes are involved in solving them.

Chapter 6, by Jean Murray and Caroline Clissold, focuses on low attainment in mathematics. It looks at the knowledge and understanding of addition and subtraction, as used in mental calculations, of a group of mathematically low attaining children. The findings show that these 9- and 10-year-olds – all of whom struggled with mathematics – could be divided into three groups according to the calculation methods they used. The chapter draws on case study data to illustrate and discuss the characteristics of the three groups: continuing counters, beginning strategists and algorithm clingers. In the latter part of the chapter Jean and Caroline argue that, in order to achieve long-term patterns of success in the subject, it is crucial that children's *confidence* and *competence* in numeracy are both raised. In other words, children need both the knowledge and understanding of the relevant facts, skills, concepts and strategies *(competence* is used here as a convenient, if somewhat limited, shorthand term for this complex network of mathematical knowledge and learning), and the *confidence* in their own ability to use and apply these things successfully.

Chapter 7 focuses on aspects of teaching mathematically promising students. Ron Casey introduces a model that has been successfully used by the Brunel Able Children's Education Centre to enhance the quality of mathematics teaching for gifted mathematicians in several local authorities. Taking account of international research and theory, issues relating to both identification of mathematical talent and strategies for provision are discussed. A number of practical ideas on design of tasks and organisational styles are provided. A range of examples of children's work and examples of resources are also provided.

In Chapter 8 Valsa Koshy and Sarah Jackson-Stevens consider issues relating to assessment of mathematical learning. They explore three specific aspects of assessment: What are we assessing in mathematics? What types of assessment should we use? How do we enhance our assessment practices and translate the principles into classroom practice? They also discuss the purposes of assessment within the planning, teaching and assessing cycle and focus on the role of formative assessment in enhancing the quality of learning. Drawing on recent research and their extensive work with teachers and student teachers, they provide a list of what constitutes good practice in assessment in mathematics.

We hope this book will help to unlock aspects of teaching mathematics and support all those who are involved in the teaching of mathematics in their different roles. We have tried to make the style accessible and the ideas practical. Theory and research underpin our writing. We hope that our book will help the reader to think about issues in more depth and make more informed decisions in their teaching.

References

DfEE (Department for Education and Employment) (1999) *A Framework for Teaching Mathematics from Reception to Year 6.* London: DfEE.

DfEE/QCA (Department for Education and Employment/Qualifications and Curriculum Authority) (1999) *The National Curriculum: A Handbook for Primary Teachers in England.* London: DfEE.

DfES (Department for Education and Skills) (2004) *Making Mathematics Count: The Department for Education and Skills' Response to Professor Adrian Smith's Inquiry into Post-14 Mathematics Education.* London: DfES.

Hardy, G. H. (2007) *A Mathematician's Apology.* Cambridge: Cambridge University Press.

Johnston-Wilder, S. and Lee, C. (2010) 'Mathematical resilience', *Mathematics Teaching* 218: 38–41.

Ofsted (2008) *Understanding the Score.* London: Ofsted.

Slavin, R. (2009) 'What works in teaching maths', *Better: Evidence-Based Education, Maths,* 2 (1): 4–5.

Williams, P. (2008) *Independent Review of Mathematics Teaching in Early Years Setting and Primary Schools.* London: DCSF.

Aspects of numeracy

Bob Jeffery

Introduction

Behind the apparently straightforward attributes of numeracy lie some rather puzzling features connected with both fundamental aspects of number and the complex historical background of present-day approaches. This chapter aims to set a context for the rest of the book by highlighting some of these aspects through a series of interactive exercises.

Numeracy comprises the knowledge, skills and understanding necessary to move around in the world of numbers with confidence and competence.

The term 'confidence' as used here implies a feeling of security, the ability to make connections between the various aspects of numeracy and the courage to develop personal methods and vary them according to the particular problem. 'Making connections' is used rather than 'understanding' as the latter term has a history of abuse in the teaching of mathematics as in 'Do you understand what I want you to do?' Many adults express quite the opposite of confidence about numeracy.

The chapter does not provide a comprehensive treatment, but the exercises are designed to help the reader build some connections between different strands and to develop a personal story about numeracy. In this respect, it is in line with the definition above. You do not become numerate without thinking for yourself and you cannot help others without some appreciation of potential difficulties.

The exercises require you to engage in mathematical thinking and to reflect on your own thoughts and experience. There is a commentary at the end of the chapter. To get the maximum benefit carry out the exercises before reading the commentary.

Exercise 1: What is number?

Number is an abstract concept.

It is unfortunate that the term 'abstract' has become almost a term of abuse in the English language. However, mathematics is a subject that deals with abstract concepts and children work with abstract ideas in their earliest mathematical encounters.

Suppose you have just arrived from another planet and you have no concept of number. You enter a world where everyone is talking about number using number names such as one, two, three . . . . What are the possible sources of confusion as you try to understand what is going on? You could start by thinking of someone pointing at a picture of three yellow ducks and saying 'three'. As far as you are concerned the word might mean *birds, yellow, dinner* or *three!* How can you learn what is meant by 'three'? See also the example in Figure 1.1.

FIGURE 1.1 Does 'Erh' mean 'two', 'red' or 'telephone box' in Chinese?

Exercise 2: Mathematics in the mind

Try the problem shown in Box 1.1.

BOX 1.1 Breaking sticks

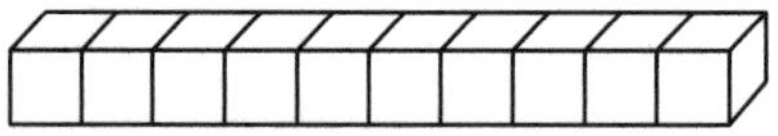

This stick of ten cubes can be broken into two shorter sticks.

Here is one way of doing it.

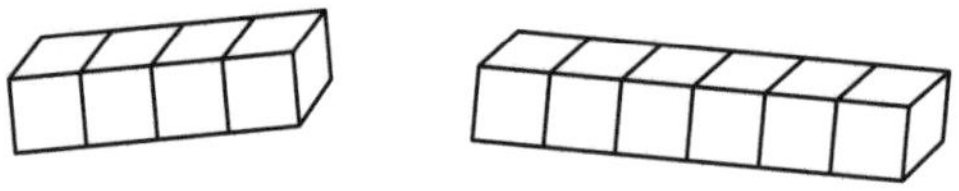

How many ways can you break a stick to ten cubes into two shorter sticks?

There are two different answers that are commonly given. What are they? Check with someone else if you can see only one answer. What is going on here and what has it got to do with the abstract? Did you stick with the physical problem or start playing with numbers?

Postscript

The picture shows the stick broken into six cubes and four cubes. The *difference* between six and four is two. Take a ten-stick and break it so that the *difference* is six. Try to do the same for differences four, eight and three. Make up a general rule about this activity. Note to what extent you rely on manipulating the cubes (perhaps in times of stress!) and what kind of thought experiments you make. Watching children do these activities will tell you quite a lot about their numeracy.

Exercise 3: Counting

Look at the exercise shown in Figure 1.2. For this exercise to be effective you *must* count the squares in each box. Review your strategies and difficulties. You may find it useful to use terms such as 'one-to-one correspondence', 'order', 'pattern', 'grouping', 'counting in . . .', 'odd and even'.

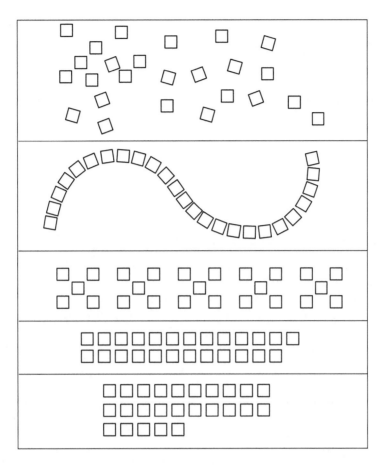

FIGURE 1.2 Counting.

Exercise 4: Fundamental ideas about number and number operations (Box 1.2)

BOX 1.2 Number and number operations

Sit down with at least one friend and a box of mixed materials – any small objects that can be used for counting. It would be useful to have materials that possess a number of different attributes such as different colour or shape.

Try to use the materials to illustrate as many of these terms as possible.

- ordinal number, cardinal number;
- counting;
- one-to-one correspondence;
- counting on and counting back;

- symbolism and numerals;
- repeated addition;
- repeated subtraction;
- sharing;
- addition, subtraction, multiplication, division;
- odd and even;
- more than, fewer than;
- grouping;
- place value;
- the difference.

Exercise 5: Mental arithmetic: an investigation

For the activity in Box 1.3 you will need at least one friend to help. The calculations should all be done mentally. There is no limit on time!

Do them one at a time and then compare notes about your methods after each one. Take your time to explore the differences fully, including the origins of your methodology, speed and accuracy, relationships with written calculations, mental images and personal feelings.

BOX 1.3 Mental arithmetic

- Add 18 and 14
- From 125 subtract 88
- 26 multiplied by 9
- 105 divided by 13
- From 152 subtract 63
- 48 multiplied by 12
- 132 divided by 4

Exercise 6: With and without place value

Life is made easier by having a place value system of numeration, both for naming numbers and calculations (Box 1.4). The Romans didn't crack this one!

BOX 1.4 Place value

A Roman nightmare

24 + 19 =   14 + 15 =   36 – 19 =

Convert these to Roman numerals, try the calculations and weep! The Hindu–Arabic system of numeration that we use offers some advantages. What are they? Discuss.

ENGLISH	CHINESE
One	E
Two	Erh
Three	San
Four	Ssu
Five	Wu
Six	Liu
Seven	Chi
Eight	Pa
Nine	Chiu
Ten	Shih
Twenty	Erh Shih
Fifteen	Shih Wu
Forty-five	Ssu Shih Wu
Fifty-one	Wu Shih E
Seventy-eight	Chi Shih Pa

What is 32 in Chinese? What is 89? How *did* you do it? The number of numbers is infinite, so how is it that we can have a name for every number? Investigate counting in some other languages. How much do you need to learn in order to count to 1000?

Exercise 7: Modelling number: place value 1

This commercially produced material (Box 1.5) is attributed to Z. P. Dienes and has its uses in helping to resolve problems about the nature and role of the place value system of numeration. Try these activities to learn something about the material and its potential.

BOX 1.5 Modelling number: place value 1

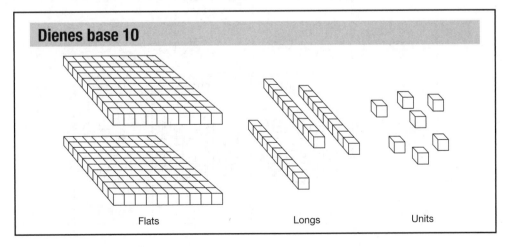

Dienes base 10

Flats   Longs   Units

Big pile

Make a big pile of wood. See if you can simplify it so that you have the same amount of wood but fewer pieces.

Cube games (for two to four players)

Take turns to throw a die. The number you throw entitles you to add that number of units to your pile. The first person to make two longs is the winner.

Everyone starts with two longs and eight units. Take turns to throw a die. The number you throw tells you how many units to take away from your pile. The first person to get to zero is the winner.

The four rules

Explore how to model the four rules with Dienes. Try 'teaching' a friend. Note issues and questions for further discussion. Look to see how some mathematics schemes approach the use of Dienes.

Exercise 8: Modelling number: place value 2

There are many materials that can be used to help resolve particular problems. Try the activities in Box 1.6 to learn something about the materials and their potential.

BOX 1.6 Modelling number: place value 2

Counting boards

Explore the use of counting boards with counters, coins, Dienes and numeral cards.

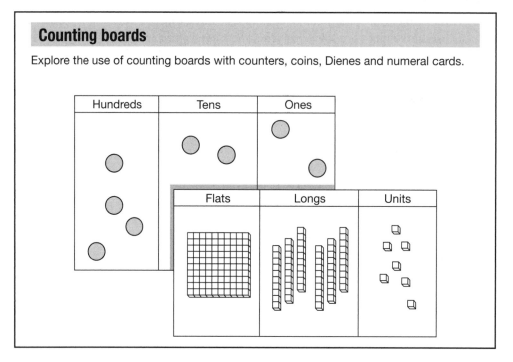

High and lows – for two players

You need a counting board and 20 cards with the numerals 0–9 (two of each). Place the cards face down. Take turns to pick a card and place it in either the tens or the units position. The second card must be placed in the remaining place. Highest number wins (or lowest number, or nearest to 67 . . .).

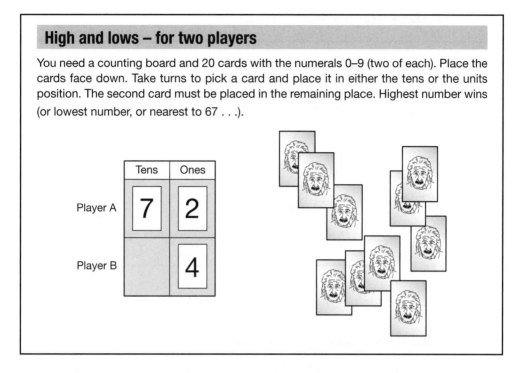

Exercise 9: Modelling number: number lines and strips

Number lines and strips are just two ways of representing ideas about number and number operations. They can be useful as physical objects or as mental images. Explore their potential by engaging in the activities in Box 1.7.

BOX 1.7 Modelling number: number lines and strips

What do these jumps on the number lines illustrate?

0 1 2 3 4 5 6 7 8 9 10 11 12 13 14 15 16 17

0 1 2 3 4 5 6 7 8 9 10 11 12 13 14 15 16 17

0 1 2 3 4 5 6 7 8 9 10 11 12 13 14 15 16 17

0 1 2 3 4 5 6 7 8 9 10 11 12 13 14 15 16 17

0 1 2 3 4 5 6 7 8 9 10 11 12 13 14 15 16 17

Make up your own.

0 1 2 3 4 5 6 7 8 9 10 11 12 13 14 15 16 17

0 1 2 3 4 5 6 7 8 9 10 11 12 13 14 15 16 17

0 1 2 3 4 5 6 7 8 9 10 11 12 13 14 15 16 17

Twenty Questions

Think of a number and give your friends 20 questions (yes or no answers).

Explore any mental images they have. Discuss the implications for teaching.

Number strips

Imagine you are folding the number....
  The crease is at 12– what does 7 land on?
  4 lands on 22– where does the crease come?

0 1 2 3 4 5 6 7 8 9 10 11 12 13 14 15 16 17 18 19 20 21 22 23 24

Exercise 10: Tables

You should be familiar with the multiplication table square (Figure 1.3) and its potential for stimulating thinking about numbers and number operations.

Investigate the patterns and symmetry – these can help in reconstructing forgotten facts.

Numbers may occur once, twice, three times or more. What is the reason?

On the next few pages there are some challenges to help you see the potential of the multiplication square.

1	2	3	4	5	6	7	8	9	10	11	12
2	4	6	8	10	12	14	16	18	20	22	24
3	6	9	12	15	18	21	24	27	30	33	36
4	8	12	16	20	24	28	32	36	40	44	48
5	10	15	20	25	30	35	40	45	50	55	60
6	12	18	24	30	36	42	48	54	60	66	72
7	14	21	28	35	42	49	56	63	70	77	84
8	16	24	32	40	48	56	64	72	80	88	96
9	18	27	36	45	54	63	72	81	90	99	108
10	20	30	40	50	60	70	80	90	100	110	120
11	22	33	44	55	66	77	88	99	110	121	132
12	24	36	48	60	72	84	96	108	120	132	144

FIGURE 1.3 Multiplication table square

Exercise 11: Building strategies for multiplication

The problem is how to learn to use the facts you know to generate the ones you don't know. Use the activity in Box 1.8 as the basis for discussion of how to set about it.

BOX 1.8 Strategies for multiplication

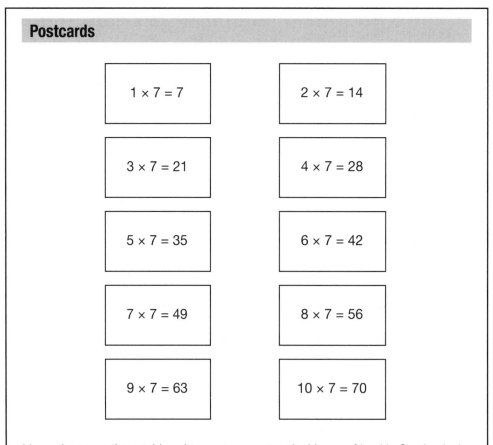

Postcards

$1 \times 7 = 7$

$2 \times 7 = 14$

$3 \times 7 = 21$

$4 \times 7 = 28$

$5 \times 7 = 35$

$6 \times 7 = 42$

$7 \times 7 = 49$

$8 \times 7 = 56$

$9 \times 7 = 63$

$10 \times 7 = 70$

I have the seven times table written out on postcards. I have a friend in Scotland who wants to know the answer to 16×7. Which postcards should I send?
What instructions would you send about what to do? Consider how you would record this. Try this with the thirty-nine times table!

Exercise 12: Using a calculator to support mental arithmetic

There are many calculator activities that are aimed at developing mental arithmetic. Review the role of the calculator in the activity in Box 1.9.

BOX 1.9 Developing mental arithmetic

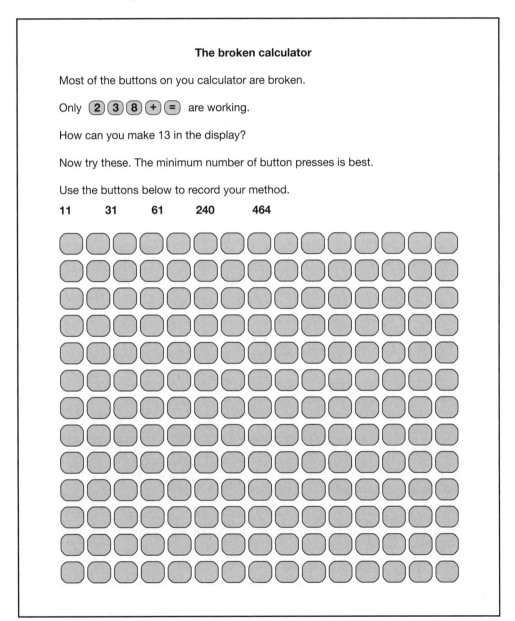

The broken calculator

Most of the buttons on you calculator are broken.

Only (2)(3)(8)(+)(=) are working.

How can you make 13 in the display?

Now try these. The minimum number of button presses is best.

Use the buttons below to record your method.

11   31   61   240   464

Exercise 13: Investigating number (Box 1.10)

BOX 1.10 Investigating number

Monitor your actions and thought processes – use this list to help you.

- being playful
- making categories
- testing conjectures
- explaining

- asking questions
- making conjectures (generalisations)
- being persistent

Sometimes true, always true, never true

Check these out and explain:

- the sum of consecutive odd numbers is a square number;
- the sum of three consecutive numbers is a multiple of three;
- the sum of five consecutive numbers is an odd number;
- the sum of two consecutive numbers is an odd number.

Consecutive sums

These numbers are made from the sum of consecutive integers:

$7 = 3 + 4$
$30 = 9 + 10 + 11$
$15 = 1 + 2 + 3 + 4 + 5$
$14 = 2 + 3 + 4 + 5$
$15 = 4 + 5 + 6$

Investigate.

Happy numbers

A number is HAPPY if the number chain made by summing the squares of the digits eventually leads to 1. For example, 23 is happy.

$$2^2 + 3^2 = 13 \qquad 1^2 + 3^2 = 10 \qquad 1^2 + 0^2 = 1$$
$$23 \longrightarrow 13 \longrightarrow 10 \longrightarrow 1$$

Of course, 13 and 10 are happy as well.
All numbers that are not happy are SAD. Find the happy and sad numbers that are less than 100.

Exercise 14: Written algorithms

An arithmetical algorithm is a procedure for calculation.

There are several different algorithms that enable the same calculation to be performed. They all exploit the powerful features of our system of numeration (Hindu–Arabic), which is based on place value.

A 'standard' written algorithm is one that is commonly used and taught. Effective 'personal' written algorithms (or variations on a standard algorithm) will also be encountered.

Teachers and schools have to make decisions about the relative importance they give to the development of standard and personal algorithms in their teaching. This is not a trivial matter to determine.

What is your view about these attributes of written algorithms (Box 1.11)?

BOX 1.11 Written algorithms

Essential, desirable, not essential – what do you think?

A written algorithm should:

- be efficient (produce answers quickly);
- be effective (produce a high proportion of correct answers);
- be understood (an understanding of why it works, not just memorisation of the processes);
- be standardised so that all children learn the same algorithm;
- be based on the mental algorithms that children use;
- be invented by the learner.

Note: This is not a list of achievable characteristics; they are in conflict with each other. The challenge is to make the best compromise and maximise the desirable aspects.

Review your opinion after working through the next few pages.

Exercise 15: What does rote learning feel like?

In Box 1.12 you are invited to learn a new algorithm for subtraction.

BOX 1.12 A new algorithm for subtraction

A new method of subtraction

$546 - 268 =$

Subtract each digit in the smaller number from 9 and write the answers under the larger number:

$546 - 268 =$
731

Add:

$546 - 268 =$
731
‾‾‾‾
1277

Remove the 1 at the beginning and add it to the last digit

$546 - 268 = 278$
731
‾‾‾‾
1̸27̸7̸8

Now try some more!

Yes it does work! But why?

Exercise 16: Written algorithms for subtraction: an exercise in morality?

This is a useful piece of historical information to help you interpret some of the subtraction algorithms you will find 'at large'. It is not a guide to how you should teach subtraction.

There are two popular written algorithms for subtraction in the adult community in the United Kingdom. They are called 'decomposition' and 'equal additions' (Box 1.13). Decomposition is favoured in schools because it permits children to develop it themselves through the use of materials (e.g. Dienes arithmetic blocks). The understanding of why equal additions works is more difficult. Sadly, equal additions is more likely to produce the correct answer – and produce it faster!

There are 'traditional mutters' that go with these methods and particularly with equal additions, with the terms 'borrowing' and 'paying back' prominent. Borrowing and paying back does not relate to *why* the algorithm works. The terms probably have their origin in Victorian strategies for remembering the algorithm by reference to well-known moral principles.

Somehow the term 'borrowing' has 'leaked' into the decomposition algorithm – with lack of morality because there is no 'paying back'! It would be sensible to use words and phrases such as 'break down the ten into ten ones', which relate more closely to what is happening.

BOX 1.13 Written algorithms for subtraction

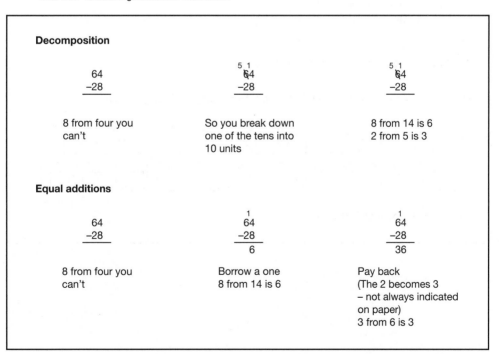

Decomposition

| 64 | ⁵ ¹ 64 | ⁵ ¹ 64 |
| −28 | −28 | −28 |

| 8 from four you can't | So you break down one of the tens into 10 units | 8 from 14 is 6 2 from 5 is 3 |

Equal additions

64	¹ 64	¹ 64
−28	−28	−28
	6	36

| 8 from four you can't | Borrow a one 8 from 14 is 6 | Pay back (The 2 becomes 3 – not always indicated on paper) 3 from 6 is 3 |

Exercise 17: The problem with division

The idea of 'sharing' develops from social activities, and many children (and adults) persist in calling division 'sharing'. Unfortunately, the development of efficient mental algorithms is based more on the notions of *repeated subtraction, division as the inverse of multiplication* and *place value*.

Look carefully at the examples in Box 1.14 and imagine that you are using the bricks to solve the problem (or use materials). Can you identify which one is 'repeated subtraction'?

BOX 1.14 Division

---

24 ÷ 6 = 4

How many 6-brick towers can you make with 24 bricks?

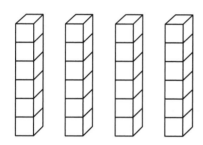

What do you count to find the answer?

Share 24 bricks equally between 6 children. How many do they get each?

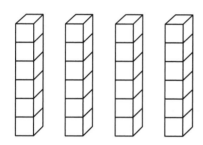

What do you count to find the answer?

Exercise 18: Some language issues

In Box 1.15 find language clues for the four rules – and look for misleading clues as well. Consider the kind of strategies that could be employed to clarify the issues – drawing pictures, visualising, materials. Discuss the implications for teaching.

BOX 1.15 Language issues

Suppose you wanted to use a calculator to solve these boring simple problems. Which of the following would you enter?

$$12 + 3 = \qquad 12 - 3 = \qquad 12 \times 3 = \qquad 12 \div 3 =$$

- There are 12 cows in a field. How many cows will be left when 3 have been taken away to market?
- In a bus there are just 12 men and 3 women. How many people are there in the bus altogether?
- If 12 sweets are shared equally between 3 children, how many does each receive?
- There are 3 houses in a road and each house has 12 windows. How many windows altogether?
- John lives at number 12 and Sushma lives at number 3. Where does Surjiben live?
- A piece of rope 12 metres long is cut into 3 equal parts. How long is each part?
- Wayne has saved up £3 to buy a game that costs £12. How much more money does he need?
- Maggie has saved up £12 to buy a football. She still needs another £3. How much does the football cost?
- Dan's pencil is 12 cm long and Maria's is only 3 cm long. How much longer is Dan's pencil than Maria's?
- How many towers 3 bricks high can you build out of 12 bricks?
- When 3 people are away from the office there are only 12 people left. How many people are there in the office when nobody is away?
- How many 3-metre skipping ropes can you make from a piece of rope 12 metres long?
- Jan has 3 cakes and each cake is divided into 12 pieces. How many pieces altogether?
- A beetle is 3 cm long and a worm is 12 cm long. How many times as long as the beetle is the worm?
- There are 12 different body colours and 3 different seat colours for a Ford car. How many different colour combinations are there?

Exercise 19: Making sense of fractions

In the diagrams in Box 1.16 the fractions are represented by area. There are many other ways of representing fractions (e.g. on number lines) and each one can help you develop your thinking about them.

BOX 1.16 Fractions

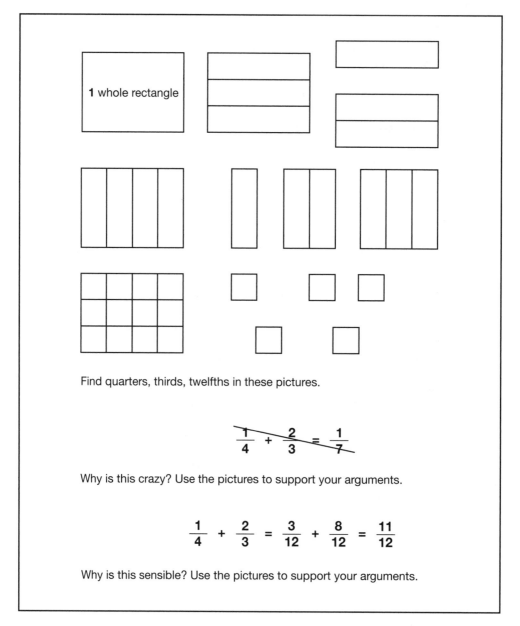

Find quarters, thirds, twelfths in these pictures.

$$\frac{1}{4} + \frac{2}{3} = \frac{1}{7}$$

Why is this crazy? Use the pictures to support your arguments.

$$\frac{1}{4} + \frac{2}{3} = \frac{3}{12} + \frac{8}{12} = \frac{11}{12}$$

Why is this sensible? Use the pictures to support your arguments.

Notes

Exercise 1: What is number?

Numbers used in this way tell us 'how many'. We call this aspect of number 'cardinality'. To learn about the cardinal number three you need to experience 'three-ness' in many different contexts. As well as cardinality, number is also used to describe order. Duck number three is the third duck.

'Erh' means two in Mandarin Chinese.

Exercise 2: Mathematics in the mind

The two common answers to the first problem are five and nine. If you count breaking into three and seven as being different from breaking into seven and three you get nine. If you count them as the same you get five. So, which is correct? Well, if you look at the words of the problem carefully and at the picture, you will see that there are nine places where the stick could be broken. If you got five, you should also be pleased because you have moved into the abstract world and temporarily forgotten about the cubes – behaving just like a mathematician! Can you predict what would happen with eleven cubes or twenty cubes?

In the second activity you should reflect on the knowledge you have had to recall in order to find the answer. You are also asked to do the impossible – make a difference of three. Can you make an argument about why this is impossible (think about odd and even numbers).

Exercise 3: Counting

The answer is five in each case although this may not be suspected at a casual glance. Counting can tell you about both cardinal (how many as in 'seven') and ordinal (order as in 'seventh'). You can count by making a one-to-one correspondence between a remembered list of names (one, two, three . . .) and actions such as pointing. Some arrangements such as the 'snake' make counting in this way easier. If you can move the objects it sometimes makes it easier – putting them into a bag as you count for example. Most people learn to count in twos. If you play dominoes you learn to count in fives. Counting in tens is quite important in our system of writing numbers. These experiences help in some of the other counts on this page.

Exercise 4: Fundamental ideas about number and number operations

Explorations like this can help to provide a secure foundation for the development of abstract thinking.

Exercise 5: Mental arithmetic: an investigation

Unless you have been rather unlucky, this should have revealed a variety of methods. Some people are more comfortable with mental methods which mirror those that they use with pencil and paper. On the other hand, others select strategies that are suited to the particular calculation. For example, some people add in order to subtract! Lurking in the background is our place value system of numeration based on ten.

Exercise 6: With and without place value

Poor old Romans! You should be able to count in Chinese because the system, based on grouping in tens, is the same as ours. It is called 'place value' because in any numeral each digit's value is determined by its place or position. For example, in 333 the first 3 means 'three hundreds', the second one means 'three tens' and the final one 'three units'. The systematic way of recording numbers in units, tens, hundreds and so on makes it easy for us to contemplate continuing the process for larger and larger numbers.

Exercises 7 and 8: Modelling value

The relative sizes of the Dienes pieces make it clear that you could be in trouble if you mistake hundreds for units! These activities are designed to explore place value in action. Some of the strategies you will use provide the basis for written algorithms.

Exercise 9: Modelling number: number lines and strips

Addition, subtraction, multiplication, division (repeated subtraction) and division with a remainder are all represented here. Many people report 'seeing' number lines when they are working on numerical problems.

Review your strategies for solving the problems with number strips. Can you refine them?

Exercise 10: Tables

This page is all about multiplication facts. Memorisation of all the results is useful, but time spent exploring the derivation of the results and the patterns they make can help you to quickly construct the ones you have forgotten.

Also, explorations like this provide activity typical of mathematical problem solving.

Exercise 12: Using a calculator to support mental arithmetic

Common criticism of the use of calculators in education is focused on the negative aspects of dependence. However, the calculator can be used to support the development of mental arithmetic strategies as these activities show.

The calculator provides the stimulus for some mental arithmetic and a means of checking answers. Note how useful it is to have some facts committed to memory and to have some ideas of what patterns to expect. In the broken calculator activity, however, it is worth checking your answers with someone else. Don't forget you can use the buttons to make numbers with more than one digit such as 238, 833 and 32.

Exercise 13: Investigating number

Arithmetic offers far more than utilitarian calculations. There are some interesting phenomena to explore. There are no 'answers' to these investigations! You have to make up your own questions and explore them. 'Consecutive sums' gives opportunities for employing a typical range of strategies. Check your own against the following list (not necessarily in order): being playful, generating results, recording results, being systematic, tabulating results, specialising (looking at particular kinds of numbers), making conjectures (about general rules), testing conjectures (to see if they apply universally), explaining.

For happy numbers you need to persist with the numbers until you are certain that they are identified correctly. Make a picture to show the sad numbers.

Exercise 15: What does rote learning feel like?

This illustrates some of the tensions on page 22. If you got the feeling that you were not in control of the situation you will understand how children might feel if algorithms are produced from nowhere. On the other hand, this, like many algorithms, is efficient and always works. If you want a clue as to why it works, crossing out the 1 at the beginning is equivalent to subtracting 1000 and adding 1 at the end is equivalent to adding 1 unit – a net result of subtracting 999. If you can work out why the first result is always 999 too big (in three-digit calculations) you have done it. How does it work in two digits?

Exercise 16: Written algorithms for subtraction: an exercise in morality?

Explore the written algorithms used by your friends for multiplication, subtraction and division. Find out about the origins of these.

Exercise 17: The problem with division

Use any insight you get from this to examine your own strategies for division.

Exercise 18: Some language issues

You will note here that some of the obvious clue words, such as 'divided', do not necessarily point to the correct operation. Collect your own examples.

Exercise 19: Making sense of fractions

This activity is designed to help you come to terms with some of the common problems and misconceptions with fractions.

2
Using and applying mathematics in Key Stage 2

Caroline Clissold and Mark Humble

Introduction

The Williams Review (Williams 2008) expressed widespread concerns about important aspects of pedagogy. The foremost concern, which was drawn from Ofsted and Primary National Strategy findings, was the need to strengthen teaching that challenges and enables children to use and apply mathematics more often and more effectively than is presently the case in many schools. 'Using and applying' has long been recognised as important in the development of mathematical thinking (Cockcroft Report 1982; DES 1989; DfE 1995). However, research shows that many teachers have found this a challenging part of the mathematics curriculum to teach (see, for example, Hughes *et al.* 2000).

Askew (1998: 159) identifies three areas within the using and applying aspect of mathematics: making and monitoring decisions, mathematical communication, and reasoning, logic and proof. The first of these areas means that children need opportunities to make decisions about the appropriate mathematics to use, and to check that these decisions are sensible. The second involves offering children the opportunity to talk, read and write about the mathematics they have used. Reasoning, logic and proof involves 'being able to make simple generalisations, hypotheses and argue through results' (p. 159).

At the heart of this aspect of mathematics is the need to provide children with well-structured learning contexts in which their existing mathematical knowledge and thinking can be applied, developed and enriched. Contexts need to be varied, motivating, challenging and capable of providing a sense of mathematical 'discovery'. As the draft of what was to be the new primary curriculum (QCDA 2010: 44) stated, children should experience mathematics as a creative activity and be introduced to its role in the world around them. The same document then went on to recommend that children develop their mathematical understanding through focused, practical, problem-solving activities in mathematical, cross-curricular and real-world contexts. Using and applying in mathematics, then, refers to the using and applying of the skills and understanding gained in mathematics within the subject itself and also within 'real-life' and cross-curricular contexts. It is often in the latter particularly that we can assess a child's true grasp of a concept as she or he applies it to a problem outside the dedicated mathematics lesson.

This chapter reasserts the importance of giving children opportunities to use and apply their mathematical knowledge and understanding through an appropriate range of problem-solving and investigative activities. It argues that knowledge and understanding of the facts, skills, concepts and strategies of mathematics (the knowledge base of mathematics) *and* the skills of mathematical thinking can be simultaneously developed and enriched through the use of appropriate learning contexts. In particular, it offers an example of how three broad types of activities – an extended number activity, integrating mathematics into other curriculum subjects and mathematical investigations – can be used as contexts for developing both mathematical thinking and knowledge in Key Stage 2. Between them these three types of activities aim to:

- develop and enrich awareness of the world of mathematics;
- show how mathematics can be used and applied through other subjects in the school curriculum;
- include opportunities for developing thinking through the processes involved in making and monitoring mathematical decisions;
- enable children to be creative in their mathematical work;
- provide links to early algebra work through the processes of pattern spotting and reasoning, proof and logic.

Examples of each of these three types of activities are outlined and discussed in this chapter.

Using and applying knowledge within a numeracy activity: Mark Humble

The teaching resource used as the starting context for all of the investigations detailed in this section is a set of carpet tiles, numbered from 1 to 100 and set out in a 100 grid (see Figure 2.1). The tiles provide opportunities for investigating 'within mathematics itself' (Askew 1998: 158). As the ideas below show, they offer a large number of ways in which children can be challenged to make decisions, to search for patterns and generalisations, to make hypotheses, to discuss and communicate their ideas and to develop simple ideas of proof. There are also opportunities for children to explore and develop their ideas about the structure of the numbers and the number operations involved.

In a study of effective teachers of numeracy, Askew *et al.* (1997) found that one of the characteristics of such teachers was the way in which they established connections within the mathematics curriculum, enabling their pupils to understand the rich and interconnected world of numeracy. The carpet tile investigations therefore offer ways of simultaneously developing knowledge of number *and* the processes that are part of mathematical thinking.

91	92	93	94	95	96	97	98	99	100
81	82	83	84	85	86	87	88	89	90
71	72	73	74	75	76	77	78	79	80
61	62	63	64	65	66	67	68	69	70
51	52	53	54	55	56	57	58	59	60
41	42	43	44	45	46	47	48	49	50
31	32	33	34	35	36	37	38	39	40
21	22	23	24	25	26	27	28	29	30
11	12	13	14	15	16	17	18	19	20
1	2	3	4	5	6	7	8	9	10

FIGURE 2.1 The arrangement of the carpet tiles '100 square'.

All of the investigations start with practical work on the carpet tiles. These starting points offer children kinaesthetic and visual experiences that are important for all learners. Additionally, they offer a different and large-scale experience of mathematics. As Potworowski (1991: 18) identifies in school mathematics work, the motto often seems to be 'think small', not 'think big', and for most children 'the field of action shrinks to a space of about 25 cm by 25 cm, heads go down, fingers grip pens, shoulders hunch up and melancholia sets in'.

Most mathematics work is not only small scale; even when purporting to be a group endeavour it is actually solitary and focused on individual achievement. In contrast, practical work with the carpet tiles offers the starting point of a large-scale, communal experience of investigating mathematics. This starting point can then be taken into smaller-scale, pair or individual work, as and when appropriate, using a printed 100 grid. The practical work becomes the starting point, and provides an interesting and relevant scaffold for the mathematical thinking.

Two teaching ideas using the carpet tiles are outlined in Boxes 2.1 and 2.2, together with some key teacher questions identified in italic. The mathematical potential within each idea is then identified and discussed.

Ways of using the carpet tiles

BOX 2.1 Multiply me

Practical work

Split the class into two equal groups. One group will observe. Each member of the other group stands on a tile, starting from 1 and making sure that all the successive tiles are used. These children are then asked to move to the tile that is their number multiplied by 2. Before any movement occurs, predictions can be made both about individual numbers and about the general pattern that will occur on the grid.

- *What will your new number be?*
- *What number will the person next to you move to?*
- *What pattern might we make on the grid?*

Once movement is allowed, it is helpful if children standing on the highest numbers move first to prevent chaos! The pattern of bodies on the grid now needs to be considered.

- *Why has this pattern happened?*
- *What operation will enable you to return to your original position?*

Using this operation the children return to their original tiles and repeat the exercise, but this time with multiplication by 3.

- *What will your new number be?*
- *What number will the person next to you move to?*
- *What pattern might we make on the grid?*
- *Why is this pattern different?*
- *What will happen if you multiply your original number by 4? By 5?*

A smaller-scale option is for ten members of the class to stand on the tiles numbered from 1 to 10, while the rest of the class observe. This option can be useful for exploring other multiples; 9 is particularly good to try.

Mathematical potential

The children are clearly working on their multiplication tables. However, at the same time, through this physical approach to numeracy work, a feeling for the divergence of multiplication is experienced. To start with, the children are standing shoulder to shoulder and as each multiplication is applied the gaps between them increase. As they spread out a pattern representing their position becomes obvious. For example, multiplication by two produces vertical columns whereas multiplication by three has a diagonal or sloping feel to the pattern. The children should be encouraged to describe and explain these patterns.

For the children to return to their original tile after multiplication requires them to divide, division being the inverse operation for multiplication. This act reinforces the purpose of inverse operations and can be built on in the next activity.

BOX 2.2 Multiply me, then multiply me again

Practical work

If you have previously been working with only a small group then swap groups now. Children assemble as before starting at 1. These children are asked to multiply their number by 3 and move to the tile equivalent to the answer and then multiply that tile by 2.

- *What will your final number be?*
- *What will your neighbour's final number be?*
- *What pattern might we make?*

The children should now be allowed to move to the final tile and, with the observers, consider the pattern created.

- *Can you describe the pattern generated?*
- *Can you explain this pattern drawing on the outcomes of the previous activity?*
- *What single operation will enable you to return to your original tile?*

Using this operation the children return to their original tiles and repeat the exercise, but this time with multiplication by 4 and 2. Clearly with this calculation some children will be forced to move off the 100 square. This does not matter but a smaller group of, say, ten could be used to develop this activity, if appropriate.

- *What will your new final number be?*
- *What number will the person next to you move to?*
- *What pattern might we make on the grid? Why is this pattern different?*
- *What will happen if you multiply your original number by 4 and then 2?*

Mathematical potential

The main fact to be learnt from this activity is that when you multiply by one number and then another it is like multiplying by the product of those numbers. This is clarified when the children are asked to look for the single operation that is the inverse of multiplying by 3 then 2. The children should realise that the inverse is to divide by 6 because multiplying by 3 then 2 is like multiplying by 6. It is also valuable to note that the pattern derived from multiplying by 3 then 2 is a combination of the patterns that were generated in the previous activity when multiplying separately by 3 and 2, that is, a combination of parallel columns with a diagonal feel – the six times table.

Using and applying knowledge across the curriculum: Caroline Clissold

It is a well-known fact that many teachers treat mathematics as a subject on its own and always teach it discretely, never really considering the possible ways that it can be brought to life and become more purposeful to children. Since the outset of Standard Assessment Tasks, there has been a gap between children's attainment in English and their attainment in mathematics, with test results in the former subject generally being several percentage points higher than test results in the latter. I have often wondered whether this gap would exist if the children had as much mathematics in their school day as they do English. Some schools not only have a dedicated daily literacy lesson, they also have extra daily time for such things as guided reading, handwriting and spelling. The children research and make written recordings of their work during their cross-curricular studies, so having another dose of English. Mathematics, however, invariably sits in that fifty-minute to one-hour slot, four or five times a week. Mathematics is not generally part of work in geography, history or art-based topics, for example, and yet it could so easily be as it lends itself beautifully to these curriculum areas – as well as to all the others. I wonder how achievement might increase if it were? We would instantly double up the amount of mathematics taught and rehearsed daily in the classroom. Then there is book week, assessment week, art week and all those other weeks that schools have and during which, in many of the schools I visit, mathematics gets the week off. Such a pity, as mathematics could play an important and tangible role in those special, worthwhile creative weeks. In this part of the chapter, then, I will be exploring some ways of effectively linking mathematics to the other areas of the curriculum.

From my experience there are two very effective ways to plan such teaching. One way would be to link mathematics work done during the discrete lesson to topic work that is planned for other parts of the day, if and when it is appropriate. The second would be to make mathematics an integral part of the topic lesson itself. Necessary skills could be taught and practised in the mathematics lesson first and then applied during the topic session.

The following ideas can be adapted to all age ranges in the primary school, but the focus of this chapter is clearly on Key Stage 2. All the ideas here have been successfully tried and tested in many a classroom from Year 3 to Year 6; they have also been implemented with primary teachers during INSET and CPD sessions in order to inspire them to 'get creative with mathematics'. This chapter is not long enough to explore all the possibilities so the focus here will be on ideas for mathematics in art, literacy and geography. Links to science and design technology are often more obvious so won't be explored, but remember to exploit the mathematics whenever you teach these subjects, particularly those that include all forms of measuring and data handling.

Mathematics in art

Linking mathematics and art is such an obvious opportunity. Children really enjoy stories so making up a storyline in which the children have to help someone out, as in this example, is a great way to engage them in anything.

Set the scene: Mr Art Istik is opening an art gallery in a couple of weeks, but unfortunately his gallery was broken into last night and some of his most valuable works of art have been stolen. He would like the children to help him by producing their own versions of these artists' work that he can hang in his gallery while the police are trying to recover the originals.

The first that he would like them to work on is Kandinsky's *Composition VIII*. You can find a copy of this work and a brief history of the artist in the National Centre for Excellence in the Teaching of Mathematics (NCETM) *Primary Magazine* (https://www.ncetm.org.uk/resources/15650).

First of all, give a potted history of Kandinsky, maybe drawing a time line to plot his birth, death and other significant times in history that the class have studied or that are pertinent to the children themselves. You could work out how long he lived, how long ago he died, how long before the children's births he was born, using a counting strategy on the time line.

Next explore the painting – what mathematics can the children see? Ideas to rehearse or introduce could include types of triangles and quadrilaterals, acute/obtuse/right angles, perpendicular and parallel lines and concentric circles. Focus on one of those areas, for example angles, and then ask the children to make a version of a Kandinsky using acute and obtuse angles, estimating and measuring them as they go along, and then add a selection of colourful quadrilaterals.

Now Art, being very pleased with what the children produced, would like them to make their own version of another famous painting that was taken, Mondrian's *Komposition*. You can find a brief history of the artist and a copy of this work in the *Primary Magazine* on the NCETM website (https://www.ncetm.org.uk/resources/16792).

Again, it is important to give information about this artist and to repeat the time line activity from above. Next discuss the mathematics of the painting, for example rectangles, area and perimeter, right angles, fractions. I have asked children in Years 3 and 4 to cut up a copy of the painting so that they have separate squares and oblongs and then to explore all the fractions they can find. I was amazed at what they found; it was a great investigation and led the children into a more concrete and complex understanding of fractions than I would have believed. They were finding how many of the smaller pieces would fit into the larger ones and saying such things as 'I can fit eight of these into this shape so this must be 1/8 of this shape', 'I've found twelfths!', 'I can get seven of these in this shape, so I have made sevenths and three of them are the same as this so this must be 3/7 of the bigger shape'. They were exploring numerous fractions of sizes that exceeded the expectations of the objective for the session. I then asked them to make their own version of his painting by arranging all the pieces to make a pattern with one line of symmetry. We did a practical session on symmetry before they did this and the results were great.

So, two paintings completed for Art. He next wanted them to do a version of a Picasso. Again we looked at a potted history of the artist. You can find information about Picasso and examples of his art in the NCETM *Primary Magazine* (https://www.ncetm.org.uk/resources/16071). We discovered that in one of his 'periods' he used to make still life displays and paint them as shapes. So the children made up still life displays from items around the classroom, looked at them in terms of the shapes they could see and drew and painted them. Some went on to rotate them as in the examples in Figure 2.2.

Finally, Art needed a sculpture or two to replace his stolen Barbara Hepworths (NCETM *Primary Magazine*: https://www.ncetm.org.uk/resources/23370). Following a similar introduction, the children then explored three-dimensional shapes. They made a sphere out of plasticine, discussed its properties and then changed the sphere to a cube, then cuboid, cylinder, cone and pyramid, each time exploring the new shape's properties of number and shape of faces, vertices, edges, whether they were prisms or not, the angles and symmetry of the faces. The pyramid was the last shape the children made. They visualised what it would look like opened up and drew this, so making a net. They cut out their net and made a pyramid; they then did the same for a cube and cuboid and some tried successfully to make a triangular prism. They worked in small groups and once they had made a few three-dimensional shapes they put them together to make a sculpture.

After they had supplied Art with all the artwork to fill his gallery (and made some great displays for the classroom) they went on to help the police find the stolen items and the culprits. This involved measuring footprints that were found at the scene and working out the height of the suspects using body ratios. They were given maps and found routes from the gallery to possible hiding places, so using compass directions and coordinates. Happily, at the end of the project, the paintings were recovered, the culprits caught and the children had a great time, learning about different artists and also different aspects of mathematics – which they remembered. I would recommend anyone to have a go at this and to be amazed at what mathematical thinking and enthusiasm for the great artists can come from it.

Mathematics in literacy

You can get so much mathematics from the stories that you read with the children; just be aware of the potential opportunities as you read them. In a book week there are great opportunities for data handling, for example lists, tables, block and pie charts and pictograms for favourite authors, Venn and Carroll diagrams for types of genre.

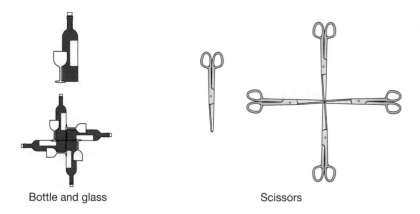

Bottle and glass   Scissors

FIGURE 2.2 Rotating the shapes.

Visiting the library and investigating numbers in the Dewey decimal system is also a good activity. In this section, however, I will focus on newspapers.

In literacy, when you are doing anything connected to report, instructional or non-fiction writing, why not encourage children to present their work in the form of a group newspaper? They could work in mixed-ability groups of around four to create their own paper to share with the class. We have done this in Year 4, but this could also work with older children – just make the instructions more complicated and raise your expectations. The children began by making up a title for their paper. They were given an alphabet code, for example a = 1, b = 2, c = 3 etc., and a maximum value for their paper's name. Next they measured and drew text boxes of specific sizes (cm, mm, mixed cm/mm) in which to stick their written work. Once they had their text boxes they measured the paper they were going to use for their writing so that it fitted perfectly into the different text boxes.

All newspapers have some form of advertising and so we asked the children to create text boxes of a specific size and make up an advert for an item in a sale. This involved fractions and percentages. They made up prices for items that they chose, and then found out how much it would be at half price, 10 per cent off etc. They added these to their newspaper. Of course there are also the TV guide and puzzle pages. So they each made a section of a TV guide using programmes that they thought would be popular, or they made up their own programmes, based on their own preferences or stories they might have read. They put their sections together, ensuring the channels were different, and together worked on a timetable, giving starting and finishing times. They also included a guide to show how long each programme would last. They tried out some of the more popular puzzles that appear in newspapers and then made up some similar ones of their own to add to their papers. An idea like this makes the real-life aspects of mathematics valid as far as producing newspapers is concerned as these are considerations made by people in the real world.

After we had done this we went on to sort out a few problems: Bobby the paper boy, for health and safety reasons, for example, was allowed to carry only 3 kg worth of newspapers at a time, and he had 240 papers to deliver. The children needed to work out how many papers he could deliver in one go, given the weight restriction, and how many trips back to the paper shop he had to make in order to deliver his allocated amount. Clearly this involved estimating and weighing newspapers. He had ninety minutes for his round, so what time did he have to leave home in the morning to get back in time to change, have breakfast and get to school for 8:45? Purposeful reasons for time work, and the possibilities, are endless.

Mathematics in geography

One of the most obvious mathematical links with geography is in country comparisons. When studying another location compare such things as rainfall, temperature, hours of sunshine and currency. These provide links with measures including time, data handling, calculation and ratio. One of my favourite mathematics/geography projects is to plan a holiday for an imaginary friend or someone who is connected to the school. When we have done this in school I begin by asking the children where they think they should advise my friend to go, so providing an ideal opportunity to collect, represent and analyse some data in the form of pictograms, bar graphs or pie charts. Quite often my friend will want to go to the same place that the children are studying, so they make up a fact file for him as they work through their topic.

Once the country has been chosen we locate it on a globe and then a world map, we measure the distance from our location, often from the capital city, and convert that according to the scale on the map to find out how far away it is. We do this in the unit of the scale and then convert to miles if necessary, because most children still think in terms of miles when travelling distances.

We explore different ways of travelling to the country and find prices of flights, ferry crossings, train journeys, whatever is appropriate. If we decide that a ferry is the best option we also calculate the cost of petrol (at current prices) for the drive to the ferry and to the final destination. From this we can advise my friend of an appropriate travel budget. Flying is usually the best option, so we will follow through that idea, although something similar can be developed for any other mode of transport.

We work out a travel plan for the person from the time they need to leave home in order to get to the airport, to give a minimum of two hours before take off, to the estimated time of arrival at their destination, taking into consideration any time differences. At this point we look at time zones and do some time work, which includes finding out the time in other parts of the world at the time it is in class.

Once the travel plan has been determined, we look at accommodation and cost this for a two-week period, adding that to the travel budget. My friend won't go on package holidays and is not too worried about the cost.

Once accommodation and travel are arranged we need to think about items that my friend should pack, so we look at the climate. This provides great opportunities for constructing and reading graphs. It is also good for looking at mode, median, mean and range of temperature, sunshine and rainfall. Once we have determined what the weather is likely to be, the children look at clothing catalogues to choose my friend some suitable items to take. We usually have a budget for this. If we think my friend might like to ski or scuba dive, for example, we make sure that appropriate clothing is chosen. This often leads us to consider baggage allowances. I have taken a suitcase filled with clothes into the classroom. The children estimate and then measure the weights of the clothes and suitcase to see if these will be within the allowance. This gives them a good visual image of how much my friend could pack.

Of course, my friend needs some local currency and so we work on currency conversions, usually through the idea of ratio, as they seem to understand this well and it involves simple mental calculation skills. We make him a ready reckoner that he can take with him, so that he can find out how much things cost in the country he is visiting and compare them with costs in England. Sometimes I ask the children to use the internet to find items that he might want to buy when he is there, such as gifts or souvenirs, and also the cost of eating out in restaurants. We then decide how much he should take for spending money – and add that to the travel budget. By the end of the project we have covered many areas of mathematics in order to plan my friend's trip; we have also found out a lot of information about the country so that my friend knows where to go, what to see and what to do.

I thoroughly recommend this way of working as the children get so much out of it. They have the opportunity to practise the mathematics they have been taught and to develop their skills in a real-life and purposeful way. In the schools that work in this way I have found that attainment rises and more importantly that children really enjoy themselves and are engaged in what they are doing.

Using and applying knowledge within investigations: Caroline Clissold

The National Curriculum originally had three strands within AT1 ('Using and Applying'): problem solving, communicating and reasoning. Problem solving required teachers to provide opportunities for children to engage in activities that promote such things as:

- making connections in mathematics and appreciating the need to use numerical skills and knowledge when solving problems in other parts of the mathematics curriculum;
- breaking down more complex problems into simpler steps before attempting a solution;
- selecting and using appropriate mathematical equipment;
- finding different ways of approaching a problem to overcome difficulties.

Communicating required children to organise their work, refine ways of recording, and present and interpret solutions in the context of the problem, and also to communicate using precise mathematical language. Reasoning required them to understand and investigate general statements, search for patterns, develop logical thinking and explain their reasoning.

Many of these requirements involve thinking skills and mathematical processes. These need teaching and rehearsing and it is often during investigations such as in the examples below that we can assess the children's development of these. The thinking skills are:

- enquiry, for example asking relevant questions, posing and defining problems, planning and research, predicting;
- reasoning, for example giving reasons for answers, drawing inferences, making deductions, using precise language;
- information processing, for example locating and collecting relevant information, sorting, classifying, sequencing;
- creative thinking, for example generating and extending ideas, suggesting hypotheses, applying imagination;
- evaluation, for example judging what is heard, read and done, developing criteria to enable this, having confidence in judgments made;

■ communication, for example sharing information, talking, listening, valuing what others say, arguing, recording.

Mathematical processes are:

■ looking for patterns;
■ working systematically;
■ identifying relationships;
■ generalising.

Try the activities in Boxes 2.3–2.5 as good examples of activities that encourage the thinking skills and mathematical processes listed above.

The culprit

The activity in Box 2.3 is a good starter activity.

BOX 2.3 Activities to encourage thinking skills and mathematical processes 1

A mathematics professor was an eyewitness to a bank robbery. Everything happened very quickly, but she was able to remember the number on the robber's T-shirt. When she got home she wrote down the number. She also wrote down some clues about it. She then gave them to her mathematics students to see if they could work out the number on the robber's T-shirt.
Can you work it out too from the following clues?

■ It's an odd number.
■ It has four digits.
■ It is divisible by both 3 and 9.
■ When it is divided by 21 there is no remainder.
■ All the digits are different.
■ The total of the first two digits is double the total of the last two digits.
■ The number is between 2999 and 5000.

Encourage the children to look for the most helpful clues to start them off and formulate their first set of parameters, for example four digits, odd number higher than 2999 and lower than 5000. They would find it helpful to know about the common rule of divisibility for 3 and 9: digit total must be divisible by 9. They can then systematically work through the numbers that are multiples of 9, for example 3681, 3627, 4761, 4815, and determine for which the total of the first two digits is double the total of the last two digits. They could use the fourth clue as a confirmation.

To be able to complete this activity the children will be using most of the thinking skills and mathematical processes. They also show that they are able to understand and investigate general statements, search for patterns, develop logical thinking and explain their reasoning (National Curriculum AT1 strand 3).

Tiles

This activity (Box 2.4) is ideal for developing all the mathematical processes. The children will be using their knowledge of square numbers, looking for patterns and finding and formulating a general rule. You could create an activity sheet with the arrangements shown on it or model using the interactive whiteboard with the children working on squared paper.

BOX 2.4 Activities to encourage thinking skills and mathematical processes 2

Set a real-life scenario for this activity around tiling a bathroom or kitchen floor or making a patio. You could give a cost for the tiles, for example white tiles cost £2.50 for packs of five and black tiles cost £2.75 for the same quantity. Say that your friend would like to make a floor/patio and he would like the children to work out the cost. He wants it to be made of square-shaped black tiles with a white surround. He would like an area of black that is twenty tiles by twenty tiles. Can the children work out how many that is and how many white tiles will be needed and then find the cost?

Begin by showing the arrangements in Figure 2.3. For the first arrangement discuss the most efficient way to work out how many white tiles there are without counting them (1 black, 8 white). Now discuss the second arrangement (4 black, 12 white). In which ways could they find out how many white tiles there are? What about the

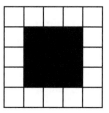

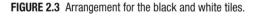

FIGURE 2.3 Arrangement for the black and white tiles.

TABLE 2.1 Recording the results of the tiles investigation

NUMBER OF BLACK TILES	NUMBER OF WHITE TILES
1	8
4	12
9	16

third arrangement (9 black 16 white)? Can they see a pattern building up? Encourage the children to work systematically, predicting first, for the next few squares of black tiles and then make up and use a rule to work out how many of each will be needed for your friend. They might find it helpful to make a table to record their thinking (Table 2.1).

Once the children have their solution they can find the cost, bearing in mind that the tiles come in packs of five so they might need to consider extra packs to account for any extra tiles needed.

This activity provides opportunities for children to engage in activities that promote making connections in mathematics, using numerical skills and knowledge and breaking down more complex problems into simpler steps before attempting a solution. It also promotes the skills of communicating through children organising their work, refining ways of recording and presenting and interpreting solutions.

The birthday party (Box 2.5)

BOX 2.5 Activities to encourage thinking skills and mathematical processes 3

Set a scenario of a friend of yours wanting to organise a party and needing some help. Alternatively you could plan a party to have in class with the children. Give the children food store and general household catalogues and ask them to choose the food they think would be suitable for a party. You will need to give them a budget to work within, for example £300, of which 2/5 is to be used for food, 1/4 of what is left for extras such as paper plates, plastic spoons, streamers and balloons and the rest for some kind of entertainment. They could work on the idea that twenty are coming and that 3/10 of them are vegetarians. You could vary the budget and fractions to suit your class.

This type of activity also makes use of most of the thinking skills and mathematical processes. For example, in sorting out the food and extras the children are using the thinking skills of information processing and reasoning by making their choices fit the budget and the needs of the guests. They will be working systematically as they decide on their choices and work out costs and how much of their budget they have left.

If you decide to have the party for the children you could organise a trip to a local supermarket to buy the things needed, as well as prepare the food, which will bring in lots of other mathematics skills.

Conclusion

This chapter has shown that knowledge and understanding of mathematics *and* the skills of mathematical thinking can be simultaneously developed and enriched through the use of appropriate learning contexts. It has shown how a wide variety of teaching contexts can be used as the starting point for the investigation of various aspects of mathematics in Key Stage 2. Such investigative work has considerable potential to develop and enrich children's awareness of the inter-related world of mathematics. It also includes opportunities for developing thinking through the processes involved in making and monitoring mathematical decisions, and communicating mathematically. Such mathematical thinking in turn links to early algebra work through the important processes of pattern spotting and reasoning, proof and logic. Finally, investigating within and beyond the subject in this way enables children to be creatively challenged in their mathematics work.

Acknowledgements

The carpet tiles ideas detailed in the first part of this chapter were originally developed by Jan Potworowski from a presentation at an Association of Mathematics Teachers conference. They have been developed by Jan and by successive generations of staff, students and teachers on INSET courses at West London Institute of Higher Education and Brunel University.

'The Culprit' and the 'Tiles' investigations were developed by Valsa Koshy and can be found in her book *Enrichment Activities for Mathematically Gifted Pupils* (2009).

References

Askew, M. (1998) *Teaching Primary Mathematics.* London: Hodder and Stoughton.

Askew, M., Brown, M., Rhodes, V., Wiliarn, D. and Johnson, D. (1997) *Effective Teachers of Numeracy: Report of a Study Carried Out for the Teacher Training Agency.* London: King's College, University of London.

Cockcroft, W. H. (1982) *Mathematics Counts, Report of the Committee of Inquiry into the Teaching of Mathematics in Schools.* London: HMSO.

DES (Department of Education and Science) (1989) *Mathematics in the National Curriculum.* London: HMSO.

DfE (Department for Education) (1995) *Mathematics in the National Curriculum.* London: HMSO.

Hughes, M., Desforges, C. and Mitchell, C. with Carre, C. (2000) *Numeracy and Beyond: Applying Mathematics in the Primary School.* Milton Keynes: Open University Press.

Koshy, V. (2009) *Enrichment Activities for Mathematically Gifted Pupils (9–11).* Twickenham: Elephas.

Potworowski, J. (1991) 'Leaps and bounds', *Junior Education,* November.

QCDA (2010) *The National Curriculum Primary Handbook.* London: QCDA.

Williams, P. (2008) *Independent Review of Mathematics Teaching in Early Years Settings and Primary Schools.* London: DCFS.

Learning effective strategies for mental calculation

Debbie Robinson

The teaching of mental calculation has been debated for decades. The Cockcroft Report (Cockcroft 1982) identified the development of effective mental strategies as being central to the mathematics curriculum. The framework for assessment introduced through the Mathematics National Curriculum in England (DfEE/QCA 1999) reinforced the importance of numeracy. Subsequent guidance for structuring and implementing the teaching of mathematics provided by the National Numeracy Strategy (DfEE 1999) and the Primary Framework for Mathematics (DfES 2003) continued to emphasis the importance of developing children's strategies for mental calculations. The impact of these initiatives in primary schools in the UK was evaluated through the Advisory Committee on Mathematics Education (2006) and again particular significance was placed on children's progress in mental calculations. Most recently the Williams Review (Williams 2008) confirmed Cockcroft's recommendations that the identification of mental strategies should retain its central position within the mathematics curriculum. Further, the Williams Review highlighted that opportunities to engage in mathematically rich practical activities and discussion about mathematical ideas are crucial to successful learning and teaching.

The high status that is given to the development of strategies for calculations within the mathematics curriculum has remained the same for decades; it can be justified for a number of reasons. Being able to calculate accurately is an obviously useful ability that can be most influential in daily life. Further, the capacity to accurately carry out mental calculations promotes greater confidence and willingness to approach other areas of learning within the mathematics curriculum. Indeed, children can apply their competence in numeracy to support their access to and progress in learning in subjects across the whole curriculum. Further, engaging in the manipulation of numbers involved in mental calculations not only strengthens children's understanding of number structures and relationships but also stimulates children to think critically and creatively in their solutions to problems.

In this chapter I intend to draw on my own practice in teaching mathematics and knowledge of how children learn and understand ideas, as well as my experiences of working with both initial training and practising teachers. I will also refer to useful research and guidance in presenting my ideas. First, I focus on two key questions:

1   What is mental calculation?
2   How can we enable children to develop effective strategies for mental calculation?

What is mental calculation?

Despite its central position in the mathematics curriculum it is difficult to find a precise definition for mental calculation. In the following section I will consider aspects of mental calculation specifically in relation to:

- the mathematics curriculum;
- written calculations; and
- how mental arithmetic might help to reveal its meaning.

How does the development of mental calculations relate to the mathematics curriculum?

Ernest (2000) identifies several 'components' that can be learnt in school mathematics. These are facts, skills, concepts and conceptual structures, strategies, and attitudes to and appreciation of mathematics. By considering these in relation to the learning of mental calculations I have attempted to establish connections between the different components of mathematics and how they might be expected to be learnt and therefore possibly taught in school. Table 3.1 attempts to summarise and structure these ideas in relation to mental calculation.

So, Table 3.1 demonstrates that mental calculation involves learning and teaching in each of Ernest's 'components' of school mathematics. In all methods of calculating children need to be able to recall memorised facts, have mental dexterity with number skills and strategies and have developed conceptual structures about number. Further, there is the necessity to structure and track methods of working (whether this is written or mental) and the need to find solutions with speed and accuracy. However, mental calculation also involves the learning and teaching of positive feelings towards and a personal connection with mathematics. These particular attitudes to and appreciation of mathematics cannot be explicitly taught in the same way as facts, skills, strategies and concepts. Rather, they are implicitly communicated through a learning environment that inspires and enables children to relate and respond enthusiastically and creatively to number.

How does mental calculation differ from written calculation?

Written calculations appear to require a consistent manner of recording workings and the adherence to a standard accepted method of computation.

For example:

Given the question 25 + 48, using a taught written algorithm, the calculation can be rewritten vertically ensuring that the unit digits are aligned from the right hand side.

$$
\begin{array}{r}
25 \\
+48 \\
\hline
73
\end{array}
$$

Understanding 25 as 2 tens and 5 units and 48 as 4 tens and 8 units is necessary to enable the numbers to be appropriately arranged in columns and subsequently added in the correct sequence. This 'layout' of the numbers allows the addition of sets of digits, moving from right to left in columns. When the 5 and 8 digits are added to total 13, the 1 is recorded below the line and the 3 to the right in the units (or ones), so that the extra ten is automatically placed beneath the 2 tens and 4 tens in the column. This allows the completion of the addition to give the answer 73.

TABLE 3.1 School mathematics: implications for learning and teaching

COMPONENT AND DEFINITION	EXAMPLE	IMPLIED LEARNING AND TEACHING STYLE
Facts are 'atoms' of knowledge	Memorisation of number bonds for addition and subtraction and facts for multiplication and division	Memorised with teacher exposition, followed by regular practice and application through problem solving
Skills are well-defined multi-step procedures	Ability to subtract two- and three-digit numbers	Mastered by exposition and modelling followed by practice and application through problem solving
Concepts and *conceptual structures* are specific properties and sets of related properties that reveal underlying meaning and interconnections	Understanding the value of a single digit '3' and then its value according to its place within the whole number system: 30, 300, 0.3, –3 etc.	Evolved and continually developed through a range of experiences including discussion, modelling, practical work, problem solving and investigative enquiry
Strategies involve informed choice of skills or knowledge in the solution of a particular problem	Deciding to add 19 to another number by adding 20 then 'compensating' by subtracting 1	Usually developed, refined and extended through modelling, discussion, practical experiences, problem solving and investigative enquiry
Attitudes to mathematics are the learner's feelings and responses	Striving for 'elegance' in the choice and application of strategies in relation to specific questions	Developed informally and implicitly by the breadth and quality of mathematical experiences provided, inspiring children to be confident and tenacious in their approaches
Appreciation of mathematics involves awareness of its value and role in life and what mathematics is as a whole	Developing ideas about infinity that are based on a genuine inquisitiveness	Developed informally and implicitly through the creativity of teacher presentation and children's responses together with opportunities to critically reflect on the learning process

In contrast, when the calculation is made mentally, there is no necessity either to resort to the use of pen and paper or to adhere to any particular method. So 25 could be considered as 20 and 5 and 48 as 40 and 8. This subtly different interpretation of the place value of the numbers involved in the written as opposed to the mental calculation methods is highlighted by Thompson (1999). Here partitioning the numbers enables the more significant numbers 20 and 40 to be added to give 60 first, followed by the 5 and 8 making an additional 13. Partitioning 13 as 10 and 3 allows the final answer to be reached by adding 60 and 10 and then the 3. However, there is no requirement to add the most significant numbers first. The mental calculator is encouraged to adopt a personalised and flexible approach, which could even involve them rearranging the numbers in the calculation to give 48 + 25, which may give a different perspective. This contrasts strongly with the written method, which dictates the order in which columns of numbers are added and the precise manner in which numbers are recorded to ensure the automatic transfer of any additional sets of tens from the units column and sets of hundreds from the tens and so on.

Further, without the requirement to classify the value of numbers into columns headed by powers of ten, each number may be considered in a wealth of different ways. So, 25 could be partitioned as 20 and 5 as well as any number of alternative combinations. These might include, for example, 10 and 10 and 5 or 20 and 2 and 3. This flexibility in the understanding of the composition of numbers encourages and allows much greater freedom in the approach to finding the answer to any given question. Without the necessity to consider numbers in terms of tens and units, a wealth of number relationships and bonds can be utilised.

In this particular example pairs of numbers that add to give 10 might imply the reorganisation of the calculation as 48 + 20 + 2 + 3. This enables counting on from 48 in twenty (i.e. 48 + 20 = 68) or in two lots of tens (i.e. 48 + 10 = 58 and 58 + 10 = 68). The remaining 5 can then be added as 2 and then an additional 3. In this way adding the 2 to the subtotal of 68 (i.e. 68 + 2 + 70) makes a complete and 'convenient' multiple of 70, which allows the remaining 3 to be added with ease to give the total 73.

So the interpretation of the place value adopted by the calculator may be an essential way in which mental calculations may differ from written calculations. The successful application of a standard written algorithm is dependent on a uniform and consistent interpretation of the place value. In contrast the freedom to choose how to partition the numbers involved (i.e. other than as tens and units) enables the mental calculator to employ their individual flexibility, choice and creativity in the possible methods of solution. Using mental calculations is essentially about the freedom to use 'informal', rather than a necessity to use 'formal', methods.

As part of my work with students and qualified teachers I have asked them to answer numerical problems in their heads, without writing anything down. They then compare and contrast their methods in order to analyse the understanding and strategies they have demonstrated. Despite the continued emphasis on mental strategies for calculating through the provision of training and guidance, as the adults explained how they had calculated the answer some confessed that they had carried out the calculation in their head, but as a written sum. They kept track of their working with a mental picture of the standard algorithm, sometimes even including horizontal parallel lines for the answer, with small 'carried' digits below. These teachers had defaulted to a method and understanding of place value dictated by written calculations. They had simply 'held' their workings in their head, rather than recording them with pen and paper.

So using a written method may not necessarily involve writing workings down. Conversely, writing workings down may not preclude being engaged in mental calculation. In fact, recording can be of great value in both the learning and teaching of mental calculations and in particular in the development of conceptual understanding and mental imagery.

For example:

The use of empty number lines would be a most effective way of demonstrating possible strategies for calculating the answer to 25 + 48.

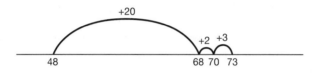

After sketching a straight line the number 48 (the larger number) is marked on the left of the 'empty number line'. Next an initial jump of +20 is made up to 68. Then the addition of 5 more is carried out by jumping +2 up to 70 (achieved using 'bridging through a multiple of ten'), followed by the final addition of 3 to give 73. Encouraging children to use empty number lines provides significant benefits. It can assist children in planning and plotting their approach. This experience supports their developing understanding of concepts, place value and number operations. It also enables them to create and retain mental visual images and eventually their capacity to calculate without the need to record with pen and paper. Further, the evidence provided by their recording on the empty number line both illustrates and illuminates their thinking processes, providing valuable diagnostic information for self-, peer and teacher assessment.

So carrying out written calculations may not necessarily involve writing workings down. Conversely mental calculations could involve the use of pen and paper to structure and keep track of approaches and indeed to make progress. The essential difference is in the opportunity to choose to think about numbers and methods with both individuality and originality.

How does mental calculation differ from mental arithmetic?

Mental arithmetic could be considered as the ability to use 'mental dexterity' in the solution of numerical problems. For example:

In order to illustrate this consider the question 16 × 15.
A reasonable method of solution might be to restructure the problem as 16 × (10 + 5).

A secure understanding of both place value and the laws of arithmetic are essential to understand this method. The distributive law allows 15 to be partitioned as 10 and 5. In this way $16 \times 10 = 160$ and then $16 \times 5 = 80$ can be calculated with comparative ease as 16×5 will be half of 16×10. Finally these products are totalled to give 240 (i.e. $160 + 80 = 240$).

The identification of helpful number relationships, together with the recall of relevant memorised number facts and the appropriate completion of number operations, allow the solution to be obtained with both speed and accuracy. The method described could be demonstrated by a child who is engaged in either mental calculation or mental arithmetic. What may be relevant in identifying a significant difference is a consideration of the child's recent learning experiences. If the particular solution to the question 16×15 followed repeated practice of this specific strategy, it is more likely that the approach has been 'implied' to, rather than 'selected' by, the calculator. In this case the teacher's planning and expectations determine the difference. Mental arithmetic may be ensured by the teacher who provides a set of similar related problems that they have equipped and prepared the children to respond to. In contrast, mental calculation can be promoted when a teacher provides a selection of varied problems and challenges them to make a thoughtful and conscious choice about how they should most effectively solve each problem.

Further, it is important to recognise that if the teacher appears to value the speed and accuracy of the answer then the children may elect to use a strategy they are more familiar and confident with. However, if the teacher explains that they are interested in how they approached each problem and the reasons for their choice the children may be encouraged to think more independently and feel liberated to think more imaginatively.

The solution to 16×15 could be found in a number of creative ways. For example:

Using its proximity to a known fact (i.e. $15 \times 15 = 225$).
As the original problem is 16, not 15, lots of 15 a further 15 is required, and so $225 + 15 = 240$.
This can also be considered as partitioning 16 as $15 + 1$, making $16 \times 15 = (15 + 1) \times 15$. In this way $15 \times 15 = 225$ and $1 \times 15 = 15$ making 240.

Alternately, the factorisation of both or one of the numbers could allow smaller products to be calculated in a more convenient order and with more ease. For example:

	16×15
becomes	$8 \times 2 \times 5 \times 3$
allowing	$(2 \times 5) \times (8 \times 3)$
making	$10 \times 24 = 240$

The preference of one approach over another will be determined by many factors and may often reveal children's experiences and their particular understanding of the number system, memorised facts, number relationships and strategies. The most 'appropriate' deployment of a particular approach is made in relation to each specific problem. There is still the desire to be efficient in terms of speed and accuracy, but an additional aspiration for mathematical 'elegance' is added: a desire to consider and capitalise on a broader perspective of mathematical relationships and systems. So mental calculation may be about *valuing the quality of the process*, as well as the *correctness of the product*.

How can we develop effective strategies for mental calculation?

My work in schools has provided me with opportunities to observe children who are very able mental calculators. Some children seem to learn effective methods for mental calculations without direct teaching or even guidance. Exactly how they acquire their abilities is uncertain. However, the majority of children will need support. To explore the nature of this support I intend to consider:

■ How can we engage children in their learning?

■ What are the characteristics of an effective mental calculator?

■ How can we plan to enable children to develop effective strategies for mental calculations?

How can we engage children in their learning?

To better understand how learners approach numerical problems I have asked groups of adults and children to memorise a specific array of numbers (e.g. Figure 3.1) in just one minute. They were encouraged to approach the challenge in any way they wished. Comparing and contrasting the methods used provides a valuable opportunity to appreciate the diversity of particular approaches and attitudes. From my experience of this evaluative process learners typically display a number of particular approaches (Table 3.2).

All of the groups of adults and children were able to reflect on their own learning process and match it with either the specific single approach or a combination of approaches. Interestingly the most confident individuals were those who took the time to search for and establish memorable connections between the numbers in the grid. This evaluation of approaches may have implications for planning for mathematical learning and teaching. So we should embrace the possibility for diversity in the manner in which:

■ teachers present ideas in their teaching;

■ children are able to respond in their learning.

9	2	7
6	5	4
3	8	1

FIGURE 3.1 Array of numbers.

TABLE 3.2 School mathematics: implications for learning and teaching – approaches to learning

DESCRIPTION OF APPROACH	EXAMPLE
Physically tracing the position of a specific sequence of numbers as they appear on the numbered grid	Linking the arrangements of numbers with physical shapes, i.e. 1, 2 and 3 from right upwards to left in a triangle
Reciting the numbers as single digits or in groups as integers	Repeatedly 'saying' and 'hearing' the numbers in their head as a series of digits, i.e. 9, 2, 7, or as groups of integers, i.e. 927
Creating and holding a mental image of the numbers as they appear on the grid	'Burning' an visual impression of the shape and arrangement of numbers, which remains after the numbered grid has been removed
Rewriting the grid at least once to assist their ability to visualise their position	Using pen and paper to replicate the numbered grid one or more times to develop a better understanding of its construction
Searching for and establishing memorable connections between numbers	Identifying relationships and patterns, i.e. starting from the horizontal sequence 927 numbers below go down or up by 3 (9, 6, 3) or (8, 5, 2) or (7, 4, 1)

Table 3.3 attempts to exemplify possible strategies for the teacher's presentation of ideas and the children's responses to learning. The obvious implications for the teacher are that planning should provide learning, teaching and assessment opportunities that reflect this variety of approaches to learning. I believe that the most tangible evidence of the benefits of this type of planning in the classroom are in the creative and effective use of resources. Resources provide stimulating devises for teachers to present ideas and powerful tools for children to manipulate independently or collaboratively. Most primary classrooms in Britain are equipped with number cards, 100 squares, counting sticks, number lines, money, dice and counters. Some choose to use considerably more. However, in contrast, schools in the Netherlands have a policy of using key resources almost exclusively. For this reason, their versatile use of the empty number line is predominant in the teaching of strategies for mental calculations involving all four operations. So, is there a possibility that planning to include variety in both teaching and learning may be confusing children? Askew *et al.* (2001) caution against the overuse of and dependence on resources. They feel that, although they can provide valuable models for clarifying and structuring understanding, ultimately children need to be able to work mentally and independently. It is therefore essential that the teacher and indeed the children understand the reasons for the selection of particular resources and their intended purpose. Drews and Hansen (2007) explain and justify the use of resources in relation to Bruner's ideas about three modes of learning. In 1966 Bruner described children's 'enactive' mode (providing physical apparatus to move and organise), 'iconic' mode (using pictures and contexts to present and represent ideas) and 'symbolic' mode (discussing and expressing with mathematical symbols and notation). Experiencing and progressing through these modes of learning enables children to build a 'storage system' that not only enables them to retrieve known information, but also supports them in their development of new ideas. So planning for children to learn

TABLE 3.3 Strategies for teacher presentation and pupil response

Strategy	Example
Doing and moving 24 37 2.5 1.945 2.75	**Order a sequence of numbers**. Putting numbers on separate cards allows them to be moved and sorted in positions relative to each other. It also encourages children to develop strategies for making comparisons, i.e. aligning digits on cards in order to match them up in tens, units, tenths etc...
Visualising and contextualising	**Negative numbers**. Children more readily understand and are able to work with negative numbers when they are placed in a familiar context, i.e. money and the notion of debt and credit or the raising or lowering of a lift or temperature gauge.
Listening and talking **2 8** **3 5** $30 + 20 = 50$ $35 + 28$ $50 + (10 + 3) = 63$ $8 + 5 = 13$	**Developing strategies for addition**. Requiring children to share resources can encourage discussion. Each pair of children makes two numbers between 10 and 99 with arrow cards. The task is to agree how to find the total of the numbers and to record their method. If one child is responsible for the units and the other the tens, the need to negotiate when the units bridge over the tens emphasises and reinforces the necessary exchange.
Recording and drawing 30 29 1 $1 \times 29 = 29$ $30^2 = 900$ 30 29 $29^2 = 900 - 29 - 29 - 1$ $1 \times 1 = 1$ 1 $29 \times 1 = 29$	**Calculating squares of numbers**. The square of 29 is very close to the square of 30 which is 900. The problem arises in knowing what needs to be subtracted. A sketch of both squares is an excellent way of establishing the precise relationship, i.e. $29^2 = 30^2 - 29 - 29 - 1$.
Patterning and relating 0 1 2 3 4 5 6 7 8 9 10 11 12 13 14 15 16 17 18 19 20 21 22 23 24 25 26 27 28 29 30 31 32 33 34 35 36 37 38 39 40 41 42 43 44 45 46 47 48 49 50 51 52 53 54 55 56 57 58 59 60 61 62 63 64 65 66 67 68 69 70 71 72 73 74 75 76 77 78 79 80 81 82 83 84 85 86 87 88 89 90 91 92 93 94 95 96 97 98 99	**Developing compensation strategies for addition**. 100 squares provide a wealth of possibilities for exploring relationships that help in the development of strategies for calculating. A counter can be placed on any number of the 100 square (most conveniently the top half). By tracking its movement when 0, 1, 10, 20 and then 9 and 19 is added, compensation strategies are illustrated and developed.

from the manipulation of tools, the presentation of images and opportunities to express and represent their thinking may be crucial in the development of mathematics.

The effective use of resources can enhance the quality of learning and teaching because:

- unstructured and structured equipment can be used to motivate children to actively participate and to provide 'tools to think with' as they are manipulated;
- visual images and contexts can stimulate interest and place learning in a meaningful setting that clarify and give purpose to learning;
- pen and paper can enable informal recording to structure and track processes and to illuminate and communicate thinking and theories.

However, the teacher must continue to justify and fully understand their choice and purpose for each of the resources they use. So if a teacher plans to place the application of mental strategies in the context of money they must consider how the use of coins, the context of money and the manner of recording learning will enhance learning and teaching:

- Will the opportunity to select and arrange coins and notes stimulate the children to think more creatively about how they partition amounts of money in order to calculate? For example, 75p could be considered as 50p, 20p and 5p pieces or three 20p pieces and one 5p piece rather than as 7 tens and 5 units without the context of money.
- Does placing the learning in a 'real-life' setting involving money give purpose and help to clarify the meaning of underlying ideas? Or is the context simply 'window dressing', which in fact overcomplicates and detracts from the actual learning intended? For example, measuring in order to create a pair of slippers can provide a relevant use of working with decimal fractions in the context of centimetres.
- When children record their learning how does the process contribute to their learning? Or does it simply provide a way of assessing their answers? For example, giving children the freedom to represent their learning journey and theories as they wish provides a 'window' to their thinking.

Used thoughtfully, resources provide a wealth of possibilities for teachers to 'model' and present ideas in a more inspiring and meaningful manner and for children to respond more actively either independently or collaboratively. Further, utilising resources promotes and stimulates discussion between teacher and children and between children themselves. This more dynamic form of teaching and learning creates more opportunities for the teacher to make informal assessments about the quality of teaching and learning throughout the lesson.

What are the characteristics of an effective mental calculator?

Children, and indeed adults, who have effective strategies for mental calculations demonstrate particular abilities, approaches and attitudes (Table 3.4). You may recognise many of these characteristics in the most able children you have worked with. It is important to note though that not all of the most able children show themselves to be effective mental calculators. Koshy (2001) advises that the abilities of 'gifted and talented' mathematicians may not always be reflected in their competence in carrying out mental calculations. They may prefer to identify methods of solutions rather than complete the actual mechanical calculation. However, this description of particular abilities, approaches and attitudes of an effective mental calculator may provide broad aims towards which all the children we teach could aspire. Further, embedded in these characteristics are implications for not only *what* should be taught, but also, as important, *how* it could be successfully taught .

How can we plan for children to develop effective strategies for mental calculations?

In my experience children's development can be enhanced by planning to aspire to the characteristics of the most effective mental calculators.

TABLE 3.4 School mathematics: implications for learning and teaching – abilities, approaches and attitudes of an effective mental calculator

ABILITIES	APPROACHES AND ATTITUDES OF AN EFFECTIVE MENTAL CALCULATOR
Rapid, reliable recall and use of key number facts	These include addition and subtraction bonds and multiplication and division facts
Strong conceptual understanding of the number system	This involves a deep and developing understanding of place value that enables the continued improvement and extension of knowledge of key number facts as well as skills and strategies for calculating
Accurate application of a range of skills for calculating	These include a variety of specific procedures for all four operations for calculating, which can be efficiently followed and performed
Flexibility strategies to solve particular calculations efficiently	This involves the desire to make informed judgment about the most effective skill to select to employ with a given set of numbers and situation
The capacity to plan and keep track of an efficient and coherently structured mental calculation	This involves the representation of a solution through visual imagery or informal written jottings
Willingness to reflect on their thinking processes through collaboration	This involves the open-mindedness to critically discuss and evaluate their own and others' ideas to improve their learning
A 'creative sense' of number that informs and inspires playfulness and tenacity	This involves an awareness and appreciation of number patterns and relationships that support trial and improvement in order to achieve the 'best' solution

Developing abilities

RECALL OF MEMORISED NUMBER FACTS

Key number bonds for addition and subtraction and multiplication and division facts need to be learnt. Developing conceptual structures relating to place value and calculations enables children to extend this core of known facts and to continue to derive others. For example, as children's understanding of place value develops, knowing the fact that $3 + 6 = 9$ enables them to derive the fact that $30 + 60 = 90$ and later than $0.3 + 0.6 = 0.9$.

Although facts are recalled individually, they are more easily remembered if relationships between them are based on practical experience of how these facts are physically built.

For example:

Using counting sticks to generate tables through repeated addition.

0	3	6	9	?	15	18	21	?	27	30

0	1	2	3	4	5	6	7	8	9	10

Then removing/concealing facts in order to highlight connections between particular facts.

Regular, ongoing repetition and reinforcement is a vital part of learning and extending known facts. It is important to ensure that this process is motivating, purposeful and appropriate for each child. Setting personal, achievable targets, in turn, of speed and accuracy is an important part of this process.

For example:

Playing games that provide stimulating and enjoyable opportunities for the short and frequent practice and application of facts.

Encouraging children to search for links between facts helps them to learn new facts and develop checking strategies.

For example:

Using known facts to derive new facts helps children to identify patterns in results.

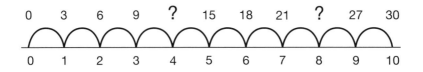

0 5 10 15 20 25 30 35 40 45 50 55 60 65 70 75 80 85 90 95 100

Children can use their knowledge of the ten times table to work out the five times table (i.e. five times a number = ½ of ten times a number).

Illustrating the relationship between two tables allows valuable checking strategies to be highlighted (i.e. five times and odd number equals an odd answer ending in 5, whereas five times any even number equals an even number ending in 0).

The value of each fact is increased if it is known and remembered in a number of different forms. This enables groups of facts be more readily applied to a wider range of situations.

For example:

$$3+5=8$$
gives $5+3=8$
as well as $8-3=5$
and $8-5=3$

Cutting up a particular number fact into five parts provides many opportunities for matching and sorting.

Write 3, +, 5, = and 8 on cards.
On the reverse of the + card, write '–' (the inverse operation) and on the reverse of the = card, write ≠ (not equal).

This allows children to explore all the possible number sentences that can be created and to decide which ones are not equal.

DEVELOPMENT OF CONCEPTUAL UNDERSTANDING

A developing understanding of place value and the laws of arithmetic underpins the acquisition and ongoing refinement of a range of facts, skills and strategies for mental calculations. Children need to develop a secure conceptual understanding of larger whole numbers, fractional numbers and negative numbers in order to continue to develop their abilities as mental calculators. The more connections children make between different aspects of their learning, the more likely they are to remember what they have learnt, apply it appropriately and build new conceptual structures. As children develop their understanding of place value they will derive more facts and increase their skills. For example, the early understanding of '3' extends to include in the meaning of the numbers 30, 300, 3000, 0.3 and –3. Similarly, knowing that $3 + 2 = 5$ leads to knowing that $300 + 200 = 500$ and also that $303 + 2 = 305$. Although children need a wealth of different learning experiences in order to develop their own conceptual structures, they need to be focused in on what key ideas could be learnt.

Reducing the number of variables in the learning situations that children encounter can help children to focus on the intended learning. While practising long division they can explore ideas about number relationships.

For example:

The number 230 could be divided in turn by several different numbers, i.e. 3, 5, 10, 12, 15 etc. This would enable the children to discover the idea that the larger the number being divided by, the smaller the answer gets.

Restricting the number of factors that change in the examples that the children tackle enables them to more easily use their results to structure and support their thinking.

For example:

A range of increasingly large numbers is divided by the same number (i.e. 56, 112, 224 etc., each divided by 15):

$$15 \overline{)56}$$

When the same number is divided into larger and larger numbers, the answers should get larger each time.

Considering how learning is presented and how children record their thinking can help children to identify and make connections.

For example:

Practising doubling can be used to highlight patterns and trends in answers. Using a number line from 1 to 20 and twenty counters, children are asked to place a counter on the line above the answer as the questions are asked.

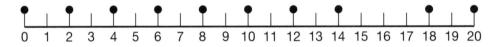

A variety of ways of asking for doubles of numbers from 0 to 10 can be used (i.e. twice zero, 1 + 1, 2 squared, two times 3, double 4 etc.).

Ask the questions in a random order and deliberately miss out one double (i.e. double 8). Ask if there is a question they think you should have asked. Finally ask the children to place the remaining counters in order to continue the pattern of doubles.

By structuring the means by which the children present their answers, the connection between doubles giving even answers is revealed and a numerical connection is made.

The hypothesis that when any number is doubled the answer is even should be justified and explained and of course tested for exceptions. Would it be possible to double a number to give an answer of 5? So does the rule only apply to whole numbers?

DEVELOPING SKILLS FOR CALCULATING

Learning experiences need to provide opportunities to gain a broad understanding of each number operation and the interrelationships between them (i.e. subtraction as the inverse of addition and multiplication as repeated addition etc.).

For example:

The recognition that addition can be about both:

(1) 'Collection' and (iii) 'Continuation'

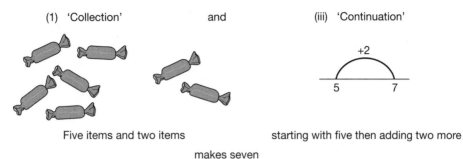

Five items and two items   starting with five then adding two more

makes seven

The choice and amount of examples used to model and demonstrate underlying concepts needs careful consideration. For example:

(a) Some teachers deliberately choose to 'confront' potentially ambiguous or complex examples early on, whereas other teachers prefer to limit the number of potential difficulties until later when children have greater experience and confidence to tackle them. There does not seem to be convincing research to support one choice over the other.

(b) In selecting the number of examples to model the needs of both the least and the most able need to be balanced. Too few examples can result in a 'whistle-stop tour' whereas explaining the same details over and over again can patronise those who are quick to grasp new learning. A solution may lie in planning to ensure the understanding of the middle and most able groups, while allowing additional time to reinforce ideas with those who may struggle. Alternately I have found that children remain engaged in whole class examples if they are allowed to answer individually or collaboratively using whiteboards. In this way children's understanding can be monitored and inform teaching.

Understanding and the acquisition of skills depend on the quality and not the quantity of practice. It is important to establish that children's understanding is correct and secure as soon as possible, and so speedy and regular feedback on their learning is essential. If a child is allowed to repeat mistakes, these errors can be extremely difficult to 'unlearn'. In my experience children need to repeat a skill at least three and no more than ten times in order to convince me of their competence. Of more value is the quality of the activity by which they are developing their understanding.

For example:

Providing a selection of questions on individual cards with answers on the back can be an effective way of managing and securing understanding through practice in a mixed-ability class. The children need to understand that it is important to get all of the answers right rather than rush and possibly make mistakes. Having the answers on the back allows children to identify any mistakes immediately. This in turn enables the teacher to identify those who need help.

DEVELOPING STRATEGIES FOR MENTAL CALCULATION

Within the skills of addition, subtraction, multiplication and division there are a number of key strategies that are employed in particular situations. There are many different taxonomies for these strategies. I will be using the list provided in the QCA document (1999) *The National Numeracy Strategy: Teaching Mental Calculations*. Being familiar with these strategies is an important aspect of planning to support children in their personal development. Children need time and opportunities to select and apply strategies in a variety of situations. The structure of this experience can differ so that (1) specific strategies are taught and then applied in different situations or (2) different situations are presented that allow specific strategies to be taught (Askew *et al.* 2001).

Strategies for addition and subtraction

Based on personal experience of working with teachers, students and children, each of the following seven strategies has been exemplified and a range of possible resources for teaching are suggested. When I tracked the development of each of the strategies through the National Curriculum (DfEE/QCA 1999) it quickly became apparent that aspects of each of the strategies are introduced from Reception through to Year 6 and beyond. Progression in learning and teaching related to these strategies is through their application; so, for example, 'counting forwards and backwards' may involve stepping on in ones or twos in the earlier years and in fractional or decimal amounts by Year 6.

■ *Counting forwards and backwards*: Early ideas about moving backwards and forwards can be established through a variety of number line activities.
  For example:

  Drop counters in a box. Ask children to keep track of the running total on their fingers or on a numbered curling snake etc.

  If nothing is added, no sound is made and the fingers stay still.

  When a number is taken out the fingers move back and so on.

■ *Reordering*: Recognising and using opportunities to rearrange the order in which calculations are carried out is encouraged when children have opportunities to visualise or actually move the numbers involved around.
  For example:

  If children generate sums by throwing dice or picking up pairs or strings of numbers on separate cards they have the opportunity to actually choose to place the cards in the order they prefer to work with them.

- *Partitioning – using multiples of 10 and 100*: Children's experiences of constructing and deconstructing numbers with arrow cards (for whole and decimal numbers) supports the development of this strategy most significantly. Challenging children to record their methods supports and reveals their thought processes.

  For example:

  Using arrow cards to generate sums encourages the idea of considering the most significant numbers first and so on.

  Examples that involve the need to exchange from tens to hundreds and so on can be used to raise issues about the suitability of this strategy for particular questions.

- *Bridging through 10*: In order to calculate up or down to a convenient multiple of ten, children need to know the number bonds that make 10. Progression in the use of the strategy depends on a developing understanding of place value.

  For example:

  Number relationships to 10 can be developed through playing games with blocks, dice and a strip of paper 10 square blocks in length. Children throw dice and collect blocks according to the numbers thrown.

  When they have a strip of 10 this is a completed tower block and they begin to build another tower.

  As children build towers they see the blocks they have so far in relation to the amount they need.

  This helps to establish both visual and numerical relationships in relation to 10.

- *Using near doubles*: Emphasising children's recall of doubles up to 10 and then to 20 gives a starting point to derive doubles of larger and decimal numbers as well as modify their doubles to consider closely related sets of numbers.

  For example:

  Developing strategies for doubling can be supported by using arrow cards to select numbers to double (i.e. 43 separates to become 40 and 3, which suggests double 4 and double 3).

  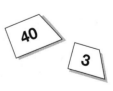

  The activity can be reversed to practise halving by working in pairs. One child secretly selects one, two or three different digit cards to make a number and then works out the double and writes down the answer. The second person halves the number in order to discover the mystery number.

■ *Compensation*: Early ideas about compensation begin with the modification of known facts to find out something that is closely related. This can be very difficult for some children. A child may work out that $5 + 2 = 7$; however, when they are asked what $5 + 3$ is they need to consider the sum as an entirely different question. In my experience, encouraging children to draw the question and then to modify this drawing by adding another one (changing the two items to a three) can help. Similarly, ways of illustrating and representing can help children to understand the notion of compensation more fully.

For example:

100 squares can be used to plot the visual, spatial and numerical effects of adding and subtracting (i.e. +0, +2, +10, +20, −0, −2, −10 etc.).

These ideas can be extended to explore the addition and subtraction amounts that are closely related to these. So +9 is seen as +10 − 1; similarly, −19 is seen as −20 + 1.

■ *Bridging through numbers other than 10*: Similar to the strategy of bridging through 10, children need to develop experience and confidence in numbers.

For example:

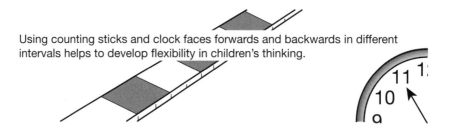

Using counting sticks and clock faces forwards and backwards in different intervals helps to develop flexibility in children's thinking.

Strategies for multiplication and division

Children's development and memorisation of multiplication facts up to 10 is essential for the development of effective strategies for multiplication and division. If children are able to generate these facts and practise them in a variety of ways they are more likely to remember and be able to apply their learning. Using their developing understanding of place value and the laws of mathematics, children can use each single known fact to derive many other facts.

■ *Knowing multiplication and division facts and using these to derive related facts*: These related facts can be generated by separating each part of the multiplication fact onto cards that can then be rearranged.

For example:

If $5 \times 9 = 45$:
(a) $9 \times 5 = 45$
(b) $45 \div 5 = 9$
(c) $45 \div 9 = 5$

- *Multiplying and dividing by multiples of 10 with whole and decimal numbers*: Encouraging estimation supports these strategies. If children are given answers they can be challenged to speculate on possible questions.
  For example:

  If 5 × 9 = 45, what multiplication fact could give 45,000?

- *Doubling and halving involving larger numbers and fractions*: Doubling and halving can be most efficient calculation strategies. It is often quicker and reliable to double and double again rather than multiply by 4. Challenging children to use only a specified group of calculations can help them to recognise the versatility and potential of doubling and halving.
  For example:

  Try to multiply each of the following numbers by 42: 12, 24 and 15.
  Allow children to only use the operations + and –, ×10 and halving or doubling.

  Note: By multiplying the same number each time the focus of the children's thinking is on finding strategies for multiplying by 12, 24 and 15.

- *Multiplying and dividing by using factors*: This strategy is often neglected, but has the potential to reduce the need for larger and potentially more difficult calculations. It relies on children's familiarity of numbers as products of different combinations of their factors. Providing practical activities supports the development of understanding.
  For example:

  (a) 15 × 9
  Writing 15 and 9 as a product of prime factors gives (5 × 3) × (3 × 3), which could then be calculated as 5 × 9 = 45 × 3 = 135.

  (b) 25 × 36 = (5 × 5) × (2 × 2 × 3 × 3),
  which reordered give 5 × 2 × 5 × 2 × 3 × 3 = 10 × 10 × 9 = 900.

  (c) 450 ÷ 18 = 450 ÷ (2 × 3 × 3), expressing the 18 as a product of prime factors. This allows divisions to be calculated in a series of small steps, so:
  450 ÷ 2 = 225 and 225 ÷ 3 = 75 and finally 75 ÷ 3 = 25.

- *Multiplying and dividing by using partitioning*: This strategy involves partitioning numbers into smaller, more manageable parts in order to be able to reorder and calculate with greater ease.
  For example:

  (a) If you did not know your five times tables you could partition 5 into smaller parts:
  5 × 9 = (2 + 3) × 9.
  Then using the distributive law (2 + 3) × 9 = (2 × 9) + (3 × 9).

(b) Similarly, if you had forgotten your nine times tables, 5×9 could be calculated as:

$5 \times (10 - 1)$, in relation to the ten times table, which is easily recalled.

So $5 \times (10 - 1) = 50 - 5$.

More usually numbers are partitioned into multiples of 10 in order to structure successive multiplications with two- and three-digit numbers. The favoured way for teaching and learning these methods is with arrow cards and the 'grid' method of multiplication.

For example:

When 25×18 is considered, arrow cards can be used to reinforce the structure of each number.

If the numbers involved are used to sketch a rectangle (possibly to scale on squared paper initially) the question is much more easily understood and calculated.

	20	5
10	10×20 $= 200$	10×5 $= 50$
8	8×20 $= 160$	8×5 $= 40$

In this way $25 \times 18 = 200 + 160 + 50 + 40$, which gives an answer of 450.

- *Multiplying and dividing by using closely related facts*: This is a sophisticated strategy with enormous potential. However, children need first to be able to identify related facts that could be of assistance in calculating and to remember to make the appropriate modification to arrive at the correct answer. Drawing can help children to make relevant connections and understand the required adjustment to be made.

For example:

(a) If you could not remember your 9 times table, you can use other related facts that you can remember and adjust the answer as required.

So 5×9 is nearly $5 \times 10 = 50$
But 9 not 10 lots of 5 are required.
So the 50 needs to be reduced by 5.
This gives $50 - 5 = 45$.

(b) This understanding can be extended to consider any number of related multiplications:

$42 \times 9 = 42 \times 10 - (1 \times 42)$;
$42 \times 8 = 42 \times 10 - (2 \times 42)$;
$42 \times 11 = 42 \times 10 + (1 \times 42)$;
$42 \times 99 = 42 \times 100 - (1 \times 42)$ and so on ...

DEVELOPING POSITIVE APPROACHES AND ATTITUDES

Part of being a mental calculator is being both quick and accurate in reaching the answer. As has been discussed, ideas about learning the required facts, skills, conceptual structure and strategies may each involve some measure of direct teaching. Acquiring positive feelings about mathematics, along with flexible and inventive ways of working, are vital to becoming an effective mental calculator. However, their development may rely more on indirect than direct teaching (Ernest 2000). So the children's development will be through the learning environment established by teachers through their own attitudes and appreciation of mathematics, the teaching and learning opportunities they provide as well as the expectation for learning they set. With pressure on the time allowed and the necessity to give the correct answer there is little incentive to take a 'risk' and try something new.

- *Role model*: A teacher's personal confidence, interest and even enthusiasm for mathematics is at the heart of the learning environment they create.
  For example:

  The increase in the use of interactive teaching methods and the provision of a variety of resources to work with has helped to portray teachers as being very 'involved' in mathematics.

- *Teaching and learning experiences*: Teaching and learning needs to embrace the breadth of mathematics and include opportunities to learn through a variety of approaches.
  For example:

  (a) If tasks are more open, longer, encourage discussion and most significantly focus on the choice of 'journey' rather then the 'destination' children are less likely to default to the safe and tested methods.

  (b) Activities need to be motivating, interesting and purposeful to engage and hold children's attention and sustain their concentration.

- *Expectations*: When children are aware that their goal for learning is the aspiration to mathematical 'elegance', expectations can be more about process than product. The self-belief and confidence to develop ideas is based on personal achievement and success.

For example:

(a) If the focus of work is on quality rather than quantity children may be encouraged to be more creative and adventurous in their work.

(b) The difficulty of the tasks must match the ability of each child and represent a personal, but attainable, challenge. This challenge might be in terms of size of number, types of operation, combination of operations, complexity or number of steps, accuracy, speed, choice of strategy etc.

Conclusion

This chapter began by attempting to distinguish mental calculations from other aspects of school mathematics. Mental arithmetic and written and mental calculations require the speedy recall of facts and accurate application of skills. The external responses from a child engaged in all these numerical activities may be the same: a single correct answer. However, I believe that it is the internal not external responses that children make that distinguish them as being engaged in mental calculations.

Becoming an effective mental calculator involves learning in all aspects of school mathematics. It therefore necessitates teaching that is not just about exposition and practice. Planning should provide opportunities for children to develop, refine and extend their thinking skills through discussion, practical work, problem solving and investigative work if they are to fully realise their potential as effective mental calculators.

Planning to teach mental calculation depends on establishing a balance in experiences and considering these ideas:

- presentation should provide clarity and purpose;
- children's modes of responses are worthwhile and contribute to their learning;
- teacher's personal confidence, interest and enthusiasm for mathematics is at the heart of the learning environment they create;
- teaching and learning opportunities that embrace the breadth of mathematics and include opportunities to learn through a variety of approaches;
- resources can provide support and structure children's thinking – use what is available;
- the nature of the activity matches the intended learning objectives and includes practice and routines, practical problem solving and investigative approaches;
- opportunities to learn independently and collaboratively through discussion are provided;
- progression is achieved through the introduction, consolidation, application and extension of areas of learning.

Above all I believe that children will make most progress when they are given the time and creative opportunities to aspire to search for the most 'economical' and 'elegant' solution possible.

References

Advisory Committee on Mathematics Education (ACME) (2006) *Mathematics in Further Education (FE) Colleges*. London: The Royal Society and Joint Mathematical Council.

Askew, M., Robinson, D. and Mosley, F. (2001) *Teaching Mental Strategies: Number Calculations in Years 5 and 6*. London: Beam Education.

Bruner, J. (1966) *Towards a Theory of Instruction*. Cambridge, MA: Harvard University Press.

Cockcroft, W. H. (1982) *Mathematics Counts, Report of the Committee of Inquiry into the Teaching of Mathematics in Schools*. London: HMSO.

DfEE (1999) *A Framework for Teaching Mathematics from Reception to Year 6*. London: DfEE.

DfEE/QCA (Department for Education and Employment/Qualifications and Curriculum Authority) (1999) *The National Curriculum: A Handbook for Primary Teachers in England*. London: DfEE.

DfES (2003) *The Primary Framework for Mathematics*. Available at http://www.nationalstrategies.standards.dcfs.gov.uk/primary/primaryframework/mathematics.

Drews, D. and Hansen, A. (2007) *Using Resources to Support Mathematical Thinking (Primary and Early Years)*. Exeter: Learning Matters.

Ernest, P. (2000) 'Teaching and learning mathematics', in Koshy, V., Ernest, P. and Casey, R. (eds) *Mathematics for Primary Teachers*. London: Routledge.

Koshy, V. (2001) *Teaching Mathematics to Able Children*. London: David Fulton.

QCA (1999) *The National Numeracy Strategy: Teaching Mental Calculations*. London: QCA.

Thompson, I. (1999) 'Mental calculation strategies for addition and subtraction, part 1', *Mathematics in Schools*, 28 (5): 2–4.

Williams, P. (2008) *Independent Review of Mathematics Teaching in Early Years Settings and Primary Schools*. London: Department for Education.

Talking about real-life mathematics

The role of ICT

John Garvey

Introduction

The Williams Review of mathematical teaching in primary schools (Williams 2008: 4) concluded that 'Two issues only are singled out: the need for an increased focus on the "use and application" of mathematics and on the vitally important question of the classroom discussion of mathematics.' The above recommendation, taken together with the enhanced focus on problem solving and cross-curricular work in primary schools, highlights the value of investigating real-life contexts that will get children talking about mathematical ideas. ICT has a prominent role to play in this, as confirmed by Ofsted (2003), which highlighted the need for regular problem-solving activities using ICT, set within relevant contexts to develop a range of mathematical skills. The need for purposeful activities set within contexts that children can relate to is affirmed by Andrews and Massey (2002: 123): 'Data, unless connected within a meaningful context and then analysed purposefully, is not worth collecting. No-one in the real world collects data for the sake of collecting data.'

It should also be noted that nobody in the real world would analyse data without the use of ICT. Data handling is one area of mathematics that lends itself to rich real-life contexts that can promote discussion. The pervasive use of the internet and online social networking has highlighted the fact that not only do we have to adjust to the world around us, but also there is a virtual world that needs to be organised and understood if we are to make sense of the 'age of information'. One important element of responding appropriately to this challenge is the need to develop in children a range of data-handling skills.

Why should children talk in mathematics?

Wickham (2008) has provided a useful summary of why children should talk in the mathematics classroom, concluding that discussion enables children to:

- engage in the process of coming to know about mathematical ideas;

- make connections between different concepts in mathematics;
- master the language of mathematics;
- work out why some methods work;
- work out why something is wrong;
- reflect upon their own thinking.

Developing capability in these important areas of mathematics has the potential to enable children to become better mathematicians. Wickham's conclusions are interesting in that they affirm Askew *et al.*'s (1998) findings on the need for children to make connections between mathematical ideas. Wickham concluded that children need rich mathematical contexts to generate talk, ideally focused on real-life contexts. The following case studies are drawn from teachers working with children within such contexts.

Key Stage 1: Farmer Giles's problem

Consider the following Year 1 play situation that was used by the teacher to develop an introduction to data handling. With reference to a toy farm that children had been playing with, the teacher explained that Farmer Giles needed to move his animals into different fields for the winter. The farmer wanted to count his animals to see how much food would be needed for the winter for each group of animals. Through whole class discussion, children came up with a range of ideas, but the one agreed upon was that if the animals were lined up they could easily be counted. Groups of children were then encouraged to line up groups of toy animals and count them (in the process developing their understanding of sets and number). To complement this they were introduced to a simple graphing program, 'Counting Pictures'. The toy farmyard was placed next to the computer and children were encouraged to use the computer mouse to 'count' the animals lined up in the farmyard – with each click of the mouse, the number of animals on screen in each column increased by one (Figure 4.1). In this way children were able to represent real objects pictorially on screen by 'telling' the computer via the mouse. Additionally, at the click of a mouse, the children proved able to explore different representations of the same data – animal pictures could be represented by coloured squares (Figure 4.1). The teacher followed up this work by using the interactive whiteboard to display the graphs, posing a range of open-ended and closed questions for children to respond to in groups:

- What do the graphs tell us?
- Tell me three things about the columns of animals.
- How many animals are there?
- How many cows are there?
- How many more cows are there than ducks?
- How many animals are there altogether?
- Could we organise the animals in a different way?

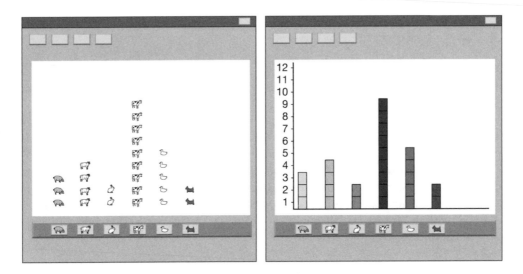

FIGURE 4.1 Farm animals: pictorial and symbolic graphical representations.

Such work draws heavily on the Primary Framework for Mathematics (DfES 2006: 73) Learning Objectives for Year 1, in which children are expected to 'answer a question and present outcomes using practical resources, pictures, block graphs or pictograms using practical resources'. Appropriate teacher questioning was critical in helping children to talk about their ideas for organising data into a form that was meaningful to them – in other words, to turn data into information.

The activity was repeated during the review session with the teacher asking the whole class 'Tell me one thing that you found out'. This enabled a range of responses from children from the very simple to a suggestion from a very able child that the farmer could use a tally method for counting the animals. The teacher asked the child to demonstrate the method to the whole class – an unexpected outcome that led to exploration of an alternative method of data collection.

The farmyard theme also lends itself to work with programmable robots. A much-loved children's story, *Rosie's Walk* (Hutchins 2009), tells the tale of a rather dim-witted hen continually walking around a farmyard in search of food. The teacher of a Year 1 class used the cards shown in Figure 4.2 (Smolkin 1999) to provide a context for collaborative work on estimating, measuring and directions using a BeeBot programmable robot as the recalcitrant hen.

Seymour Papert's (1993, 1994) espousal of his programming language Logo and associated programmable robots as 'objects to think with' has genuine resonance for teachers and children alike. Straker and Govier (1996) have suggested that children begin to 'program' (plan a sequence of actions) when they are very young, for example when they are planning the sequence of moves in a game. The use of programmable robots can be very beneficial for young children as they have the potential to be 'body syntonic' (Ainley 1996), enabling children to relate the movement of the robot to their own bodies, allowing them to take ownership of the control of the robot as a precursor for more formal programming with Logo.

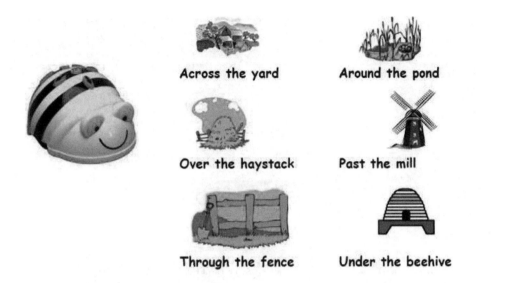

Across the yard	Around the pond
Over the haystack	Past the mill
Through the fence	Under the beehive

FIGURE 4.2 BeeBot's farmyard challenge.

Logo also has the potential to enable children to talk about, understand and develop ways of representing their understanding of mathematical concepts such as estimation, shape, space, direction and angle. The following work by a student teacher (Parry 2000) with Year 1 children illuminates this. She chose to use Pixie (a small programmable robot with a simple keyboard that allows children to select distances and left or right turns) to investigate concepts of number, direction and programming. The robot was 'changed' into an aeroplane and children were challenged to 'fly' it from house to house across a world map. Initially children were happy to work on a trial and error basis in enactive mode (Bruner 1966, 1971), commanding the robot to move from house to house. When challenged to 'fly the route in one go' the children decided, through discussion, that drawing a map of the route would be useful – representing information in iconic mode. More able children in the class were able to internalise and represent the route the aeroplane would take in a symbolic manner (see Figure 4.3).

A major benefit of programmable robots is their potential for enabling cooperation between children in the solving of problems and the opportunities they afford for children to talk about mathematics. Consider the following interaction, in which children were prompted by the teacher to demonstrate their emerging understanding about number, direction and programming:

Teacher: 'Pixie almost got there. What instructions will need to be changed?'

Imogen: 'She has to take the end one off' (*indicating that the last instruction has to be changed*).

Gagondeep: 'Yes and put another forward one on instead.'

Caitlin: 'No, I need to do six of them (*forward*) because I didn't actually make it there.'

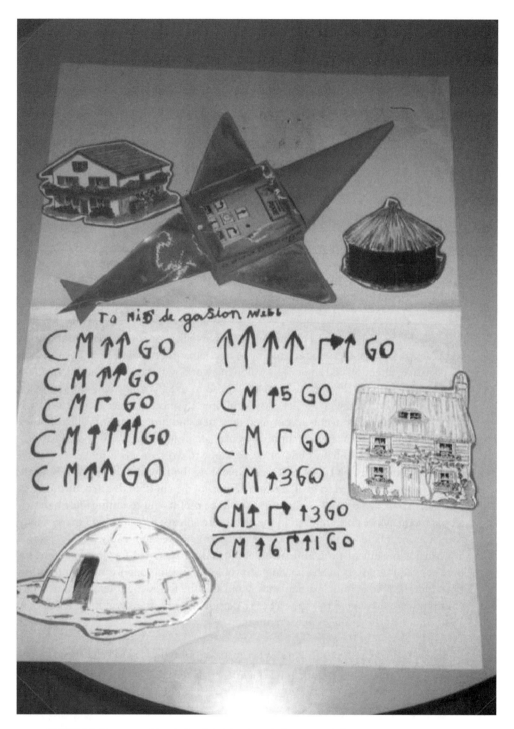

FIGURE 4.3 Programmable robots: pictorial and symbolic representation.

Teacher: 'So then what do you want to do?'

Caitlin: 'Then I want to go that way.'

Teacher: 'Right?'

Caitlin: 'Yes, right and then after right, then that way. Up one and then that way.'

This could be classified as *cumulative talk*, 'in which partners build positively upon what others have said' (Mercer 1995: 104). Such purposeful talk is not only valuable in itself, but is also an important precursor to *exploratory talk*, which has the added dimension of children engaging critically with the contribution of others.

The activity provided ample opportunities for the teacher to model the use of the language of direction of movement and was reinforced by the use of display cards in the classroom that emphasised such vocabulary.

Such work with young children on programmable robots is also critical in enabling them to develop sophistication at a later stage in using Logo as a programming tool, allowing them to break down complex problems into subtasks, viewing mistakes not as disastrous, but as an integral part of the learning process, not just within mathematics, but across the curriculum. Work with Logo has the added potential of allowing children to enter 'microworlds' (Papert 1993) in which they can explore and talk about concepts of shape, space and angle in challenging and rich contexts.

Key Stage 1: Cuddlies' picnic

This distinction between data and information was built upon by another Year 2 teacher in a context that was interesting and relevant to the children – that of a cuddlies' (cuddly toys') picnic. The teacher told her children that a picnic was to be organised for the children's teddy bears or cuddlies, explaining that, in order to make the trip a success, some planning was necessary. This was introduced through a whole class carpet session, drawing upon the principle of enabling children to identify the needs of others. The first step was for children to bring in their own cuddlies to help personalise any choices they would make. Children were then asked to work together in small groups to identify what their cuddlies would need for their picnic. Responses varied from food and drink, to umbrellas and a tablecloth. One useful category of need identified by the children was that of sandwiches. The teacher then asked each child for their cuddly's sandwich preference and then let them place their soft toy in a single undifferentiated central pile. The teacher asked the children to identify the sandwich that each cuddly wanted. The children found this impossible, as the pile of data (cuddlies) they were confronted with did not yield any useful information (organised data). Through open-ended questioning, the teacher was able to elicit from children a way of organising the data into a form that would enable them to make decisions about the number and type of sandwiches needed. Those children familiar with the idea of organising objects into sets and lining up suggested that they could place the cuddlies in lines, which the teacher supplemented with real jars of jam, peanut butter and pieces of cheese to label each column. Further work was done in organising the cuddlies into sets in different ways based on the use of Venn diagrams to display sandwich preferences that would overlap two sets (e.g. a cuddly who wanted a cheese and ham sandwich).

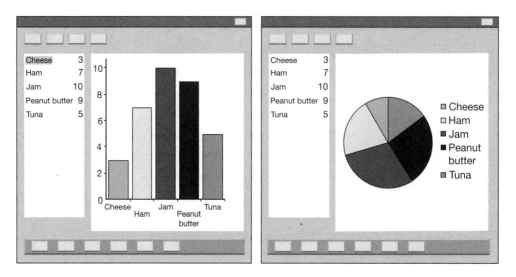

FIGURE 4.4 Sandwich preferences: selecting the most appropriate graph.

At this point the teacher introduced children to the graphing program 'Counter'. This allows children to type in data in columns and then allows those data to be converted into graphical form. The children were told that they could use the computer to store lots of data and present them in ways that would help them to plan for and answer questions about their picnic. Printouts from the graphs derived from Counter were used as a focus for teacher questioning. Children also used the printouts to show the sandwich makers (parents) the range of sandwiches needed for the picnic. The children were then asked about which graph the parents found most useful in helping them to decide the number of sandwiches needed for the picnic. They reported that parents found the bar chart easier to use as the pie charts gave no indication of the number of sandwiches in each category (see Figure 4.4).

The teacher commented that the children were developing a variety of data-handling skills:

- organising data into information in a real context;
- using the vocabulary of data handling;
- understanding the need to give the computer accurate information;
- organising and representing data in different but meaningful ways;
- realising that the computer can help in storing data and presenting it in different ways at the click of a mouse;
- discovering that some ways of representing information are more useful than others.

Such skills are precisely those that are espoused by the *Primary Framework for Mathematics* (DfES 2006: 73): 'Answer a question by collecting and recording data in lists and tables; represent the data as block graphs or pictograms to show results; use

ICT to organise and present data.'

Bruner (1957, 1971) stressed the vital role of the adult or 'experienced other' in supporting and extending children's developing understanding of the world around them, characterising intelligence as the ability to 'go beyond the information given'. Through questioning, working with relevant contexts and the judicious use of ICT, the teacher helped children to develop and express their understanding at different levels. Bruner distinguished between three modes in which knowledge is expressed or represented: enactive, iconic and symbolic. The data-handling and programmable robot work here exemplifies these modes. The enactive mode is defined by action and practical activity – in this case by children physically organising the animals and cuddlies into different categories and (in the case of sandwich preferences) labelling those categories with real objects. ICT was used to support the development of the iconic or pictorial representation of categories – the value of different forms of iconic representation was explored though open-ended questioning by the teacher using the computer printouts of graphs. The database also proved valuable in enabling children to see the way in which symbols (squares in this case) could be used to represent pictures in the graphical representation of animals, thus supporting children in understanding that data can be represented symbolically. Wood (1990: 183) makes the point that Bruner's conception of 'knowledge representation is that the representation created must bear a one-to-one correspondence with the event or activity that it depicts'. The instantaneous manner in which the categories could be represented in iconic or symbolic mode on screen was of real value in helping children to see the correspondence between different ways of representing mathematical knowledge.

Such progression in data handling also exemplifies Bruner's concept of the 'spiral curriculum' in which concepts are revisited at increasingly more complex levels of sophistication. As Bruner (1966: 27) claims, 'any subject can be taught effectively in some intellectually honest form to any child at any stage of development'. Two student teachers (Trier 1999; Lawrence 1999) accepted the challenge laid down by Bruner in their work on data handling with a Year 1 class. They were keen to find a way for children to develop their own personal records, incorporating a small range of field names (headings), with a view to exploring data handling using a card index-type database (First Workshop). They asked children to record data about themselves pictorially and symbolically by developing a 'passport' for each child (Figure 4.5)

From these 'passports' one can see that Bethan is aged 4, has blue eyes, size nine feet and blond hair, and likes beans on toast. The teachers entered the children's records into the database and, with support, children were able to identify their own records in the data file and derive simple graphs from the data. The graphs were displayed and used as a basis for simple open-ended questioning by the teachers.

An interesting twist on the concept of the spiral curriculum was observed in teacher use of the graphical data on sandwich preferences. Whilst a Year 6 class was lined up for assembly, their attention was drawn to the graphs in Figure 4.4, which were prominently displayed in the corridor next to the school hall. The teacher posed the following questions and followed them up in class-based sessions:

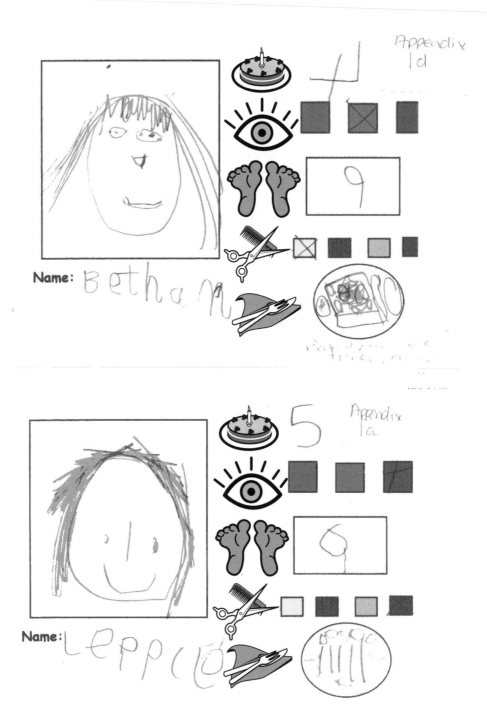

FIGURE 4.5 Card index-style record for data file.

- What is the difference between the columns?
- What is the mode?
- What is the mean?
- What is the median?
- Estimate the percentage of cuddlies who prefer cheese sandwiches.

Questioning strategies such as these demonstrate that the simplest of graphical representations can be used to challenge children's thinking about and understanding of mathematical terms in relation to the *Primary Framework for Mathematics* guidelines for organising and interpreting data. The strategy of using odd moments such as when children are lined up waiting to enter the class or assembly is perhaps one that has much to offer in terms of revisiting and reinforcing children's understanding of key elements of mathematics such as vocabulary. Murray (2002) has stressed the vital role that an understanding of vocabulary plays in the development of mathematical capability.

Key Stage 2: Exploring number with branching databases

Considering the ease with which children can master the principles of creating hierarchical or branching databases, it is surprising that they are not used more often in schools. A Year 4 class were given the challenge of categorising numbers according to their properties. Initially the numbers were kept small (from 1 to 6) and pairs of children were given digit cards and asked to sort them away from the computer in as many ways as possible. Then they were introduced in the ICT suite to the branching database 'Flexitree', with the teacher modelling the construction of a file based on categorising animals. Within a short space of time, pairs of children were able to produce their own branching database (Figure 4.6).

The teacher then displayed this file, constructed by a pair of children, on the interactive whiteboard and requested of the class, 'Tell me one thing about this file'. The open-ended nature of the question and the paired discussion strategy used enabled a rich cumulative dialogue between the children, with observations made concerning:

- the validity of the questions used – 'the best question is, "Is it an odd number?", because it really sorts out the numbers into equal groups and makes it look sort of balanced – ours was really lopsided' and 'well – that question about "Is it bigger than 4?" is a bit lame';
- where larger numbers might go – 'I think 10 would be next to the 1 because it is even, but not a prime number'.

Such discussion indicates that children are thinking hard about the properties of numbers. Research by Brown and Wragg (2001) has indicated that children rarely engage in questioning that moves beyond routines and procedures ('Do I need to write the learning intention?'). A major benefit of the use of branching databases is that they require children to ask questions about the objects to be used and even, as indicated above, have the potential to engage children in commenting about the quality of questioning used by their peers.

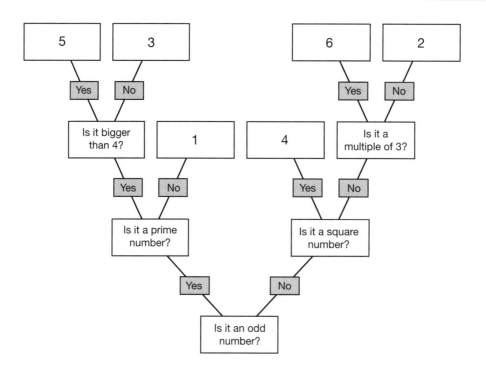

FIGURE 4.6 Sample of branching database file based on number.

As Williams (2008: 4) observed: 'Only by constructive dialogue in the medium of the English language in the classroom can logic and reasoning be developed – the factors at the very heart of embedded learning in mathematics.'

Key Stage 2: Crime scene North London (Whodunit)

Such activities as the branching database work involve categorisation, a skill that can be further developed through filtering data using a spreadsheet. The current popularity of TV crime programmes such as *CSI: Crime Scene Investigation*, in which detectives have to sift through a mass of data to solve crimes, can provide an involving context for work in mathematics. A teacher of Year 5 children introduced a crime scenario by bringing in a cauliflower that had been dyed pink using red food dye, explaining that the children would need to dissect the 'brain' of a victim of a gruesome unspecified crime. Links were made to *CSI*, which, despite its being broadcast post-watershed, all children had detailed knowledge of. After a group of children sliced open the 'brain', with incredible relish, using a fairly blunt kitchen knife, the teacher introduced a witness statement from a recent crime (admittedly mild in comparison with those shown on television), 'The Stolen Bicycle' (one of a series of crime scenarios produced under the title *Whodunit* by MAPE in 2001) (Figure 4.7). Stress was laid on the strategies used by detectives, that is, the need to work in teams, communicating with each other, and a heavy reliance on ICT.

The task involved close reading of the witness statement by children in pairs with a view to identifying clues that could be used to identify the suspect: a foreign,

Crime number 3.1

Witness No. 1:	Surinder Kaur (Schoolgirl), Age 10, Height 1.25m
Sherlock Homes:	How was your bike stolen?
Surinder:	As I was coming home from school a woman jumped out in front of me causing me to stop. She yelled at me in a language that I couldn't understand, and when she grabbed my bike there was nothing I could do to stop her stealing it.
Dr Watson:	Did you notice anything about her?
Surinder:	The blonde haired woman looked older than my mummy who is 32, but much younger than my granny who is a pensioner.
Sherlock Holmes:	Can you remember any other distinguishing features about the thief?
Surinder:	She was wearing dark glasses.
Sherlock Holmes:	Thank you for your assistance, I'm sure that we will be able to use the police computer to track down the thief.

WHO STOLE VICTORIA'S BICYCLE?

FIGURE 4.7 Whodunit witness statement.

blonde-haired woman, wearing dark glasses, older than thirty-two but younger than sixty.

The following example of exploratory talk (Mercer 1995), in which children engage critically with the contribution of others, was recorded by the teacher:

Kylie: 'Well, it must be someone really old because it says she's a pensioner.'

Jamie: 'No – have a look – it says that she's younger than her granny – her granny's the pensioner.'

Kylie: 'Well, how old is a pensioner?'

Jamie: 'Dunno – I think it's about 65 – let's put that in.'

Kylie: 'Well, she's also 1.25 metres tall – look at the top.'

Jamie: 'Don't be stupid – that's the height of the witness.'

The exchange shows the value of talking through evidence and seemed to justify the teacher's choice of grouping children of 'near ability', a strategy espoused by Askew and Wiliam (1995) in their analysis of grouping children in mathematics. Having identified clues as to the identity of the suspects, the children then used a spreadsheet to filter the original list of fifty-one suspects to six blonde, foreign females (Figure 4.8).

This allowed the children to identify Steffi Braun as the likely suspect, once the age of female pensioners was established. The teacher also invited one of the groups to use the interactive whiteboard for interrogating the spreadsheet – a promising strategy for heightening motivation, which was followed by the group explaining their findings during the plenary/review.

It should be noted that the teacher was alarmed by the draconian punishments suggested by children for the bike thief, which ranged from being imprisoned for at least a year ('Yeah, and throw away the key' – an example of cumulative talk) to being placed in a stock in the middle of town 'like in the olden days' and pelted with bicycle parts.

Key Stage 2: Evaluating fruit salads

Spreadsheets also have great potential as a tool for modelling mathematical situations. Large numbers can be manipulated easily and repeated calculations can be explored with a view to identifying patterns within number investigations. A major problem is finding situations that require the need for simple formulae at a level that children will understand. Cross-curricular work can be fruitful in this regard. Take the case of evaluating products in design and technology. In this case, Year 4 children were evaluating a range of fruit salads, including one they had made themselves. They were

Name	Surname	Sex	Age	Height(M)	Hair	Passport	Features	Blood
Sonnie	Bakker	Female	60	1.75	Blonde	Dutch	Glasses	O
Steffi	Braun	Female	44	1.71	Blonde	German	Glasses	A
Patricia	Bryant	Female	41	1.79	Blonde	None	Perfume	A
Lucy	Smith	Female	55	1.68	Blonde	None	Smoker	A
Mary	Walsh	Female	41	1.8	Blonde	None	Earring	A
Rose	Wilson	Female	33	1.9	Blonde	None	Earring	A

FIGURE 4.8 Whodunit spreadsheet showing crime suspects after filtering.

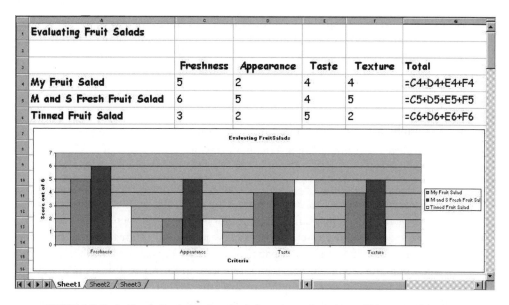

	Freshness	Appearance	Taste	Texture	Total
Evaluating Fruit Salads					
My Fruit Salad	5	2	4	4	=C4+D4+E4+F4
M and S Fresh Fruit Salad	6	5	4	5	=C5+D5+E5+F5
Tinned Fruit Salad	3	2	5	2	=C6+D6+E6+F6

FIGURE 4.9 Evaluating fruit salads using simple formulae and graphing within a spreadsheet.

guided in the development of formulae and graphs by the teacher as part of a whole class ICT session (see Figure 4.9).

The benefit of introducing children to the construction of such a table is that it can be used as a template in a variety of investigations across the curriculum. In a subsequent design and technology investigation into carrier bags, the children were able to independently use a similar table to record their evaluations of the strengths of a variety of paper bags. Similarly the template for the table used here proved useful in a range of science investigations including the testing of durability of a range of fabrics and the varying speeds of cars travelling down ramps at different angles. Through such investigations children can be led to an understanding of the value of mathematics and ICT applications in genuinely involving contexts.

Key Stage 2: Think of a number

During the numeracy hour, a Year 5 teacher was investigating mental maths problems based upon such statements as 'I think of a number, double it and take away 2'. As part of work on algebra, she incorporated such problems into the main teaching sessions involving the use of pencil and paper methods. She employed the strategy of making the problems increasingly long-winded. When signs of boredom and exasperation started to surface, she introduced the idea of using a spreadsheet to ease the process of number crunching. Introducing spreadsheets to children can be a daunting process for teachers as the cell interface presented on screen can seem far from user-friendly and there is significant potential for children to become confused about the construction of formulae. Bearing this in mind, the teacher employed an approach that has a strong tradition within the teaching of mathematics, but which has been formalised as an integral part of the National Curriculum for Design and Technology – that of focused tasks. A focused task is one that enables children to develop and practise skills as a precursor to using that skill to solve a problem. Using the school computer suite, the teacher introduced the children to the use of increasingly sophisticated formula on a column by column basis (see Figure 4.10):

1   I think of a number;

2   I add 6 to that number (first operation);

3   I multiply that number by 4 (second operation);

4   I take away the number I first thought of (result);

5   What is the number I started with?

The focused task approach involved breaking down the problem into small steps. The activity lent itself well to differentiating work by the adjustment of the complexity of the formulae presented to children. Such work can be of great benefit in allowing children to investigate number patterns in a relatively painless manner and as an introduction to the use of symbols (cell references) in formulae. When children were reasonably confident in using simple formulae, the teacher invited them to comment on the advantages of using the spreadsheet. The most pertinent comments ranged from 'it's fun to highlight the numbers and drag them down and watch the numbers come up' to 'after you put the formula in the computer does the work for you'.

Key Stage 2: Pocket money

In the following year, the teacher involved children in a survey of pocket money. They were then invited to make a choice between the following arrangements. Over a six-month period they could accept either:

1   £2 a week *or*

2   1p for the first week, 2p in the second week, 4p in the third week, 8p in the third week etc.

	A	B	C	D
1	**Number**	**First operation**	**Second operation**	**Result**
2	1	=A2+6	=B2*4	=C2-A2
3	=A2+1	=A3+6	=B3*4	=C3-A3
4	=A3+1	=A4+6	=B4*4	=C4-A4
5	=A4+1	=A5+6	=B5*4	=C5-A5
6	=A5+1	=A6+6	=B6*4	=C6-A6
7	=A6+1	=A7+6	=B7*4	=C7-A7

FIGURE 4.10 Using formulae in a spreadsheet.

The majority of children initially opted for the first option, estimating that this would yield the most cash. They were then challenged to work out whether they had made the correct choice, with some preliminary work done with paper and pencil. Most children could quickly see that they had made the wrong choice. To ease the process of repeated multiplication, children were then allowed to use calculators and guided in the use of formulae within spreadsheets (see Figure 4.11). Calculators proved effective in this regard, with children surprised at the exponential growth of wealth in the second option. However, the visual nature of the growth of numbers within the spreadsheets proved to be captivating – the prospect of receiving over £300,000 a week after six months led some to comment that they would try to secure such a deal with their own parents.

The principle of an involving context, appropriate scaffolding of the task by the teacher and using the computer to ease the process of calculation proved to be of genuine benefit in exploring how numbers can surprise and inform. The National Numeracy Strategy (DfEE 1999: xx) recommends such approaches to work in mathematics:

Where teaching is concerned, better numeracy standards occur when teachers:

- devote a high proportion of lesson time to direct teaching of whole classes and groups, making judicious use of resources such as ICT to support teaching, not replace it;

- use and give pupils access to resources, including ICT, to model mathematical ideas and methods.

	A	B	C
1	POCKET MONEY PROBLEM		
2			
3	Week number	£2 a week	1p now (x2)
4	1	2	0.01
5	=A4+1	=B4+2	=C4*2
6	=A5+1	=B5+2	=C5*2
7	=A6+1	=B6+2	=C6*2
8	=A7+1	=B7+2	=C7*2
9	=A8+1	=B8+2	=C8*2
10	=A9+1	=B9+2	=C9*2
11			
12			
13	26	52	335544.32

FIGURE 4.11 Pocket money problem.

Conclusion

Williams (2008) has stressed that it is vital that children work within mathematical contexts that they can relate to and understand. The analysis of teachers' work in this chapter demonstrates how dedicated professionals with a keen understanding of the potential of ICT have provided children with contexts in which they can develop skills of representing, organising and interpreting information with a view to deepening their understanding of the world around them. Central to teaching and learning were strategies such as the appropriate use of open-ended and closed questions, the focus on children talking through mathematical ideas, the planning of practical mathematical activities embedded within tasks involving the use of ICT and the conscious encouragement of different modes of representing information. The range of contexts investigated here is not intended to be definitive. For example, the role of calculators in enabling high-quality dialogue has not been explored because of wordage constraints. With the current highly prescriptive primary curriculum it is essential for teachers to exercise their imagination in designing contexts to extend the boundaries of children's thinking and understanding of mathematical concepts, complemented and informed by the judicious use of ICT.

References

Ainley, J. (1996) *Enriching Primary Mathematics with IT.* London: Hodder and Stoughton.

Andrews, P. and Massey, H. (2002) 'Curriculum opportunity and the statistics of lines', *Mathematical Teaching*, 181: 121–127.

Askew, M., Brown, M., Rhodes, V., Dylan, W. and Johnson, D. (1998) *Effective Teachers of Numeracy in Primary Schools: Teachers' Beliefs, Practices and Pupils' Learning.* London: University of London, King's College.

Askew, M. and Wiliam, D. (1995) *Recent Research in Mathematics Education.* London: HMSO.

Brown, L. and Wragg, E. (2001) *Questioning in the Primary School (Successful Teaching).* London: Routledge.

Bruner, J. S. (1957) 'Going beyond the information given', reprinted in Anglin, J. M. (1973) *Beyond the Information Given.* New York: W. W. Norton.

Bruner, J. S. (1966) *Towards a Theory of Instruction.* Cambridge, MA: Harvard University Press.

Bruner, J. S. (1971) *The Relevance of Education.* New York: W. W. Norton.

DfEE (Department for Education and Employment) (1999) *National Numeracy Strategy.* London: HMSO.

DfES (Department for Education and Skills) (2006) *Primary Framework for Mathematics.* London: HMSO.

Hutchins, P. (2009) *Rosie's Walk.* London: Red Fox.

Lawrence, J. (1999) 'The use of information handling software in the teaching of mathematics and science'. Unpublished paper. London: Brunel University.

MAPE (2001) *Whodunit Special.* Newman College.

Mercer, N. (1995) *The Guided Construction of Knowledge: Talk amongst Teachers and Learners.* Clevedon: Cromwell Press.

Murray, J. (2002) 'Numeracy and low attaining children', in Koshy, V. and Murray, J. (eds) *Unlocking Numeracy.* London: David Fulton.

Ofsted (2003) *Mathematics in Primary Schools: Ofsted Subject Report Series 2000/01.* London: HMSO.

Papert, S. (1993) *Mindstorms.* Cambridge, MA: Perseus Books.

Papert, S. (1994) *The Children's Machine.* Cambridge, MA: Basic Books.

Parry, E. (2000) 'Programmable robots: a small scale study', unpublished paper. London: Brunel University.

Smolkin, L. (1999) 'Rosie's Walk Activity Card'. Available at http://www.teach.virginia.edu/go/wil/Rosies_Walk_Activity_Card.pdf.

Straker, A. and Govier, H. (1996) *Children Using Computers*, 2nd edn. London: Nash Pollock.

Trier, O. (1999) 'Using ICT to support learning'. Unpublished paper. London: Brunel University.

Wickham, L. (2008) 'Generating mathematical talk in the Key Stage 2 classroom', in Jober, M. (ed.) *Proceedings of the British Society for Research in International Learning in Mathematics*, June: 115–120.

Williams, P. (2008) *Independent Review of Mathematics Teaching in Early Years Settings and Primary Schools*. London: HMSO.

Wood, D. (1990) *How Children Think and Learn*. Oxford: Basil Blackwell.

Websites

http://nationalstrategies.standards.dcsf.gov.uk/
http://www.ictopus.org.uk/
http://nrich.maths.org
http://primary.naace.co.uk/

Developing problem-solving skills in mathematics

Rachel Fairclough

The ability to solve problems is at the heart of mathematics.

(Cockcroft 1982: 73)

Over twenty years ago the importance of problem solving within the teaching of mathematics was overwhelmingly apparent and often not present within the classroom practice of many teachers. The development of the role of problem solving in the mathematics classroom was an essential aspect of applications of teaching and learning through the National Numeracy Strategy (NNS) Framework (DfEE 1999) in England. One of the major five strands in the NNS is entitled problem solving. More recently there has been an increased emphasis on children developing learning and thinking skills, whilst recognising the importance of play-based and active learning. The content of this chapter will include aspects of learning and teaching and their relationship to practical issues within the classroom teaching of problem solving. A selection of different types of problems will be presented as examples throughout. There is limited literature available from research into problem solving that focuses on the exact teaching strategies that generate improved problem-solving approaches in children (Askew and Wiliam 1995). Starting with the premise that the skill or ability defined as 'problem solving' can be taught or trained at an early age, undoubtedly the careful contribution of the class teacher will show an improvement in the time taken, breadth of skills and confidence when a child is presented with a novel problem to solve. In addition, access to material on the internet, computer games and national and international testing have contributed to the status of problem solving today.

In this chapter I will consider the following aspects of problem solving:

- the establishment of problem solving in the school curriculum;
- issues arising when teaching problem solving – an analysis of problem solving in practice;
- whether problem solving can be taught – and the teacher's role when training children to solve problems effectively;
- monitoring progress in problem-solving skills.

These issues will be viewed from different approaches – some well established, others based on personal observation and shared teaching experiences, but largely based on enriching mathematics learning throughout the school curriculum.

A definition of problem solving

The initial stage of defining 'problem solving' requires an understanding of what a problem is and when a problem can be considered solved. An understanding of both of these aspects is essential for any teacher of mathematics to ensure that appropriate problems are presented to individual children. This chapter will examine eight different problems I have regularly used in mathematics lessons and make suggestions for teacher use, including guiding children towards an appropriate conclusion. In the Cockcroft Report, problem solving is defined as 'an ability to apply mathematics to a variety of situations' (Cockcroft 1982: 73). A more recent statement for the proposed programme of learning under the heading 'Essential Knowledge' is that children should build secure knowledge of the range of ways mathematics can be used to solve practical problems (QCDA 2010). Both these definitions, written almost thirty years apart, are applicable to the types of problems described in this chapter and the approach used to analyse them. I have considered the mathematical skills required for each problem in parallel with the skills and procedures attributed to solving any type of problem, including those not obviously mathematical in structure. The most recent programme of study for mathematics in the National Curriculum (DfEE/QCA 1999) is subdivided into mathematical understanding of number operations and calculation, money, measures, geometry and statistics, and each problem in this chapter will refer to a particular aspect of mathematics.

Development of problem solving

As a result of generally accepted thinking on teaching mathematics at the start of the 1980s, investigational work, not problem solving, was introduced into primary and secondary schools in this country. The time spent on such activities varied from once a week in the most enthusiastic schools to once a year in some parts of England. The activities were sometimes overly contrived and even isolated from the mathematical skills that a child had experienced during the same year. The early experiences of investigative work were at best well integrated and relevant to child experience in all areas of the curriculum but at worst an 'add-on' activity, part of the year's work as required when teaching from the National Curriculum. Teachers who were taught problem-solving strategies and skills using mechanistic methods when they were children had to make a shift in their own thinking and mathematical practice. I found that I had to make many changes in my teaching of investigations. The project approach, collating knowledge in an attractive presentation, was not specific enough to allow definition of the precise mathematical skills and knowledge used, nor was it flexible enough to allow experience of the range and variety of strategies or processes. Therefore a more careful scrutiny of the extent to which essential strategies and processes could be taught was necessary.

Although in recent years an investigation is usually described as a type of problem, the terms – 'problem' and 'investigation' – have considerable overlap in interpretation. Children in the UK aged 16 years studying for a General Certificate of Secondary Education (GCSE) level in mathematics, at the end of Key Stage 4, have not had a compulsory investigative coursework element since 2008.

Problem solving today

The National Curriculum Attainment Target 1, 'Using and Applying Mathematics', included investigational work as an essential part of teaching at Key Stages 1, 2, 3 and 4, throughout the compulsory years of schooling from 5 to 16 years (DfEE/QCA 1999).

Each Programme of Study (PoS) in the National Curriculum begins with a relevant breakdown of how 'Using and Applying Mathematics' should be taught. These sections are further subdivided into three parts: problem solving, communicating and reasoning. I constructed Table 5.1 by counting the number of separate teachers' guidance 'bullet points' for each of the three parts. Before reading my comments about the contents of the table make a judgement yourself on the allocation of bullet points at each Key Stage for each PoS. Note that 'number and algebra' have been replaced by 'number operations, calculations and money', 'shape, space and measures' have been replaced by 'measures and geometry', and 'handling data' has been replaced by 'statistics' (QCDA 2010).

Table 5.1 indicates little change from Key Stage 3 to Key Stage 4 but the highlighted rows clearly indicate how problem solving develops across the age groups within each PoS. The three parts or strands used to define the teaching of 'Using and Applying Mathematics' cannot be separated. Although the strand called problem solving is the only one referred to in this chapter, communicating and reasoning are an integral part of any solution to a problem. As an illustrative example, the numbers in the table indicating reasoning skills increase dramatically at Key Stages 3 and 4. This reflects the

TABLE 5.1 An analysis of the 'Using and Applying' section for each Programme of Study in the National Curriculum (DfEE/QCA 1999)

PROGRAMME OF STUDY	PROBLEM SOLVING, COMMUNICATING OR REASONING	KEY STAGE 1	KEY STAGE 2	KEY STAGE 3	KEY STAGE 4
Number and algebra					
	Communicating	2	4	3	5
	Reasoning	3	2	4	4
Shape, space, measures					
	Communicating	1	3	4	4
	Reasoning	2	1	7	6
Handling data					
	Communicating		2	3	3
	Reasoning		1	3	3

phase when geometrical proofs become part of the curriculum for shape, space and measures. The examinations taken in England at age 16 years from 2012 will have a few marks allocated towards assessment of a student's communication skill.

Can problem solving be taught?

Such explicit guidelines within the National Curriculum (see Table 5.1) and the National Numeracy Strategy for teaching problem solving suggest to a teacher that problem solving can be taught in the mathematics classroom. However, my experience indicates that many problem-solving strategies develop through 'training' rather than teaching. The training situation occurs when learnt mathematical skills and latent thinking processes are applied and used in response to a particular type of problem. It is relevant at this point to examine the approaches to problem solving used by different researchers into mathematics education.

Early in the devolvement of problem solving in the mathematics classroom, Leone Burton (1986) stated that problem solving cannot be taught. An interesting statement within a book containing a wealth of interesting problems for children to solve, each problem requiring, according to Burton, no more skills than the child already has. An emphasis is placed on nurturing the natural curiosity of children, starting at their own level of understanding and by using questioning techniques to elicit skills, already present, to solve similar problems.

For example:

How many handshakes take place between twenty people if everyone shakes hands once?

The role of the teacher in this situation may be to present the problem in such a way that the curiosity aroused in the individual child will generate a solution to the problem. If the solution is not immediately forthcoming, the strategies and application of current mathematical skills will help to focus and maintain 'procedures' essential to the process of solving any problem.

The 'procedures' used to solve the problems are described in the book itself. Burton suggests a three-part approach: 'entry', 'attack' and finally 'review–extension'. The three-part approach is further subdivided into thirty-two precise actions; for example 'work backwards' is part of the attack and 'communicate' is part of the review–extension. Comparisons with the terms used in the National Curriculum document suggest that the definitions of some terms have evolved in both interpretation and status. Such a detailed analysis (Burton 1986: 26) may make a challenging checklist of actions for both teacher and child but undoubtedly allows the 'procedures' to be located, categorised and developed. Different strategies labelled 'skills' are listed under five different headings (Burton 1986: 27). For example, 'Skills for Handling Information' are often referred to as 'process' skills, whereby a process can be applied to a novel problem and a solution will be the result. A process skill for handling information is 'Sorting and Ordering'.

It is the strategies, the mathematical skills or 'tools' that can be taught, that enhance the teaching environment within which problems may be more easily solved. The timing of teaching mathematical skills may vary. The teaching can take place before the introduction of the problem or the problem can be adapted to allow learning to take place during the stages leading to the final solution. Please note that I am not referring to the process as a skill, although the processes listed later in Table 5.7 have many similarities with the skills Burton described. However, my own feeling is that the five skills stipulated by Burton – handling information, representing a problem, enumerating, finding patterns and testing – are an essential part of the training process but underpin the 'procedures' she describes. The skills she describes are strategies too. The five skills are further subdivided into fifteen subcategories. Both the skills and procedures used in Burton's book are replicated in an adapted form in many texts used in schools, even the guidelines for GCSE coursework. I have compared the two approaches in Table 5.2.

It is apparent from the allocation of skill or procedure to each of the GCSE statements that the skills taught in primary school are essential for achieving at any level in the examinations taken nationally at 16 years of age. The procedures defined as essential to problem solving at the primary age group are again indicated to be crucial to the problem-solving process needed for later examinations.

The skills I am using when describing the eight problems in this chapter are pure mathematical skills and are an indispensable part of problem solving.

What is a problem?

The definition of a problem needs to be considered before continuing the description of methods used in the classroom. How would you define a problem?

From the studies discussing teaching and learning of problem solving in school-based mathematics, the main issue arises from establishing a mutually agreeable definition of a problem. The literal interpretation of the word 'problem' from the Greek is 'a thing thrown forward', usually defined as 'put forward as a question for discussion', but the 2001 version of *The New Oxford Dictionary of English* (Pearsall 2001) has specific references to the use of the word in physics and mathematics: 'an inquiry starting from given conditions to investigate or demonstrate a fact, result, or law', or more specifically referring to games and puzzles 'an arrangement of pieces in which the solver has to achieve a specified result'. Both definitions are applicable to the type of problem solving taking place in classrooms today, and imply a need for more than one definition of a problem. A more productive approach to understanding what constitutes a problem in the mathematics classroom might include an analysis of different types of problem.

Even the skills and procedures suggested by Burton (1986) vary depending on the nature of the problem itself. Most classifications describe only four types of problem (Askew and William 1995). These four classifications will be used to define the selection of problems used in this chapter (see Figure 5.1):

1 *standard problems* are often called word problems and require interpretation before the application of mathematical operations;

2 *non-standard problems* are problems that may not have an already defined procedure (see Burton's description of 'procedure' above) for finding a solution;

TABLE 5.2 A comparison between the approach suggested for GCSE coursework investigations and the approach suggested by Burton for primary school problem solving

RECOMMENDED GCSE TEXTBOOK (KENT 1996)	LEONE BURTON'S SKILL (S) OR PROCEDURE (P)	
Make sure you understand the problem	Explore the problem	P
	Define terms and relationships	P
	Identify information	S
Check to see if you have worked on a similar problem. If you have try to make use of this experience	Try related problems	P
	Use one solution to find others	P
Try some simple and special cases	Try particular cases	P
	Focus on one aspect of the problem	P
	Test a hypothesis	S
Plan your work in an ordered way	Be systematic	P
	Sorting and ordering	S
	Choose a mode	S
	Scan all possibilities	S
Record what you are trying to do	Recording information	S
	Using a representation	S
	Many of the 'attack' procedures belong here	P
Record your observations	Develop the recording system	P
	Presenting information	S
	Recording information	S
Use appropriate diagrams and forms of communication	Translating between representations	S
	Partition the problem into cases	P
Record and tabulate any findings and results	Formulate and test hypotheses	P
Predict what you think may happen and test it. This is called testing a conjecture	Communicate	P
	Presenting information	S
	Scan all possibilities	S
	Recognising patterns	S
	Predict from a pattern	S
	Test a result	S
Try to find and make use of any counter-examples		
Generalise, especially in symbols, if you can	Make a generalisation	P
Comment on your generalisations		
Explain and justify your generalisations		
Try to prove any generalisations		

3   *real-world problems* require careful selection of relevant material and a 'model' to help manage the given information before producing a solution;

4   *puzzles* are problems requiring unusual approaches to their solution.

Occasionally a problem will fall into more than one single classification.

Askew and Wiliam (1995) found that most research in the United States has focused on standard problems whereas the UK research focuses on non-standard and real-life problems as part of the National Curriculum development work. More recent work in the UK has a focus on functional mathematics or mathematics that has a direct application to 'real' situations (for an example see Problem 6). A literature search would show very little established research evidence reviewing types of teaching strategies precipitating readily defined skills in problem solving, and the findings from the eight problems quoted in this chapter are from a small sample. In addition, research to date indicates little evidence linking the effects of problem-solving skill acquisition and child attainment both in mathematics and in other areas of the school curriculum. Askew (1998) attributes some of these results to the type of problem: Is it routine or is it realistic?

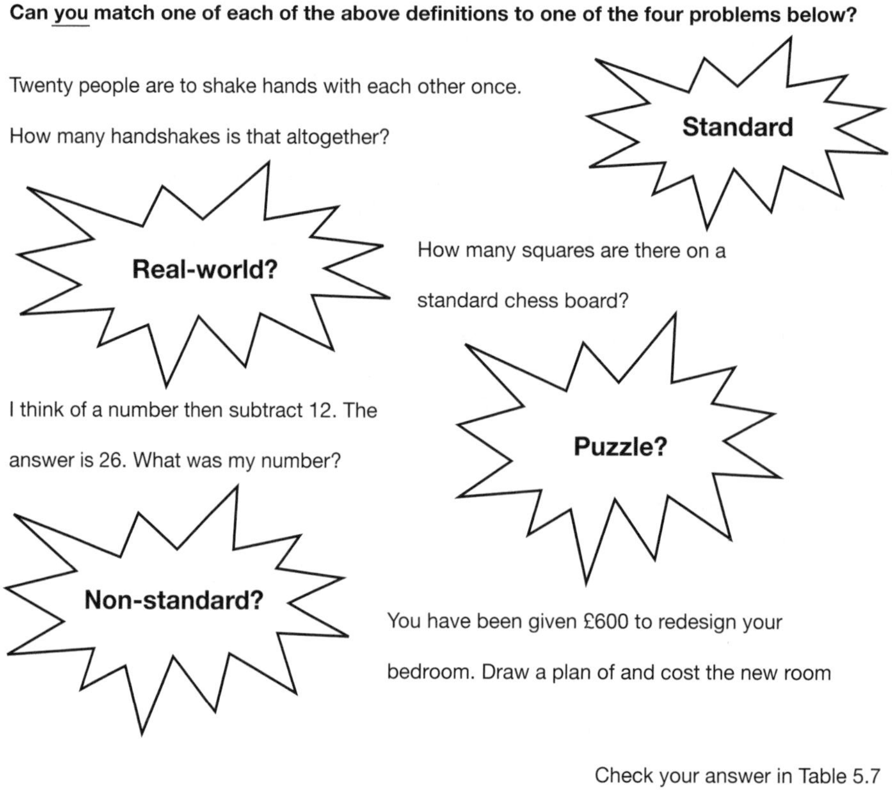

Can <u>you</u> match one of each of the above definitions to one of the four problems below?

Twenty people are to shake hands with each other once.

How many handshakes is that altogether?

Standard

Real-world?

How many squares are there on a

standard chess board?

I think of a number then subtract 12. The

answer is 26. What was my number?

Puzzle?

Non-standard?

You have been given £600 to redesign your

bedroom. Draw a plan of and cost the new room

Check your answer in Table 5.7

FIGURE 5.1 A matching activity between four problems and the four main classifications of problem types.

What is a realistic problem?

Routine as opposed to realistic problems at primary level provide many challenges over the teaching of problem solving (Askew 1998). Assuming the skills needed and the procedures acquired to solve problems are transferable from mathematics to other curriculum subject areas the teaching of the procedures, skill practice and the pleasure of problem solving could be effectively implemented in many primary schools even with the constraint of one mathematics session per day. The challenge will be how to maintain the opportunity for this transfer of learnt strategies into the secondary school years, when teachers in different curriculum areas may not communicate on a regular basis. Routine problems of the nature described by Askew are unlikely to be encountered anywhere else except in mathematics classes, although the skills and procedures may be used in a variety of circumstances.

Non-routine problems involve 'curious' problems, a mixture of non-standard problems and puzzles; the most stimulating are usually 'real' and may be encountered in other subjects and real-life situations.

For example:

How many 2p pieces will be needed to make a stack as tall as you?

The non-routine and realistic problems are the ones that encourage a child's engagement in a task, thus encouraging any potential problem solver to approach similar challenges positively.

The preceding sentences would provide convincing reasons for problem solving to be an integral part of every school curriculum, allowing each child to develop an unique repertoire of skills and procedures that may be used both inside and outside the mathematics classroom. I have observed a variety of different activities relating to arranging 1p and 2p coins as successful charity fundraising events. The mathematical skills involved are mainly money and measures but certainly engaging for the children.

The 'transfer' of problem-solving strategies

I have attempted to summarise the information discussed so far and created seven 'advantages' of problem-solving training. These are listed in Table 5.3 and teachers may notice a resemblance to learning objectives. Using the list in Table 5.3 try to note any curriculum subject area, apart from mathematics, that uses the strategies listed in the first column. Part of the table has been filled in for you, but you are free to disagree.

How many did you find? Five, six? At least one of the advantages listed in the left-hand column is used in more than one curriculum area. Many of the National Curriculum Programmes of Study use the advantages labelled B–G. This 'reciprocated' situation may enhance progress in mathematics and in non-mathematical subjects as transfer of those strategies, either skills or procedures, may be encouraged at every relevant opportunity.

TABLE 5.3 A checklist of the advantages developed through problem solving in mathematics and their relationship with other curriculum areas

ADVANTAGE OF USING A PROBLEM-SOLVING APPROACH THE PUPIL:	EXAMPLE OF CURRICULUM SUBJECT AREA
A. Uses arithmetic operations appropriately	
B. Realises that a multi-solution approach may be effective and one answer may be only part of the whole solution	
C. Considers the context of the problem not just the calculation	
D. Incorporates estimating and approximating strategies as an integral part of the approach	D. Playing rounders . . .
E. Regularly employs checking and re-evaluating strategies	
F. Interprets and analyses facts and data	
G. Uses a range of oral skills; special vocabulary, reasoned debate and discussion prompted by both provided and discovered evidence	G. English, role play . . .

Some problems

Recent research indicates that problem-solving skills are closely related to thinking skills. Try the following task for yourself before reading any more.

Task 1: How many squares are there on a standard chessboard?

Allow yourself five minute to work out the answer to the task, mentally. Only write the number of squares as your answer.

All of the responses in Table 5.4 are appropriate for the problem set and may be experienced by any person, including children in primary school presented with a problem. There are several answers; the 'correct' answer depends on the way that the question has been interpreted. The teacher is probably essential during the presentation of a problem for generating confidence within each child and directing children towards understanding the type of problem itself. I believe some more examples of problems actually used in the mathematics classroom will help explain some of the practical aspects of trying to solve problems.

An analysis of problem solving in practice

The following problems are appropriate for children studying at Key Stages 1 and 2 (5- to 11-year-olds) and accompanying descriptions of the mathematical skills and processes involved in their solution. A detailed analysis of the problems can be found

TABLE 5.4 An analysis of some different answers to the 'chessboard problem'

NOW TICK THE THOUGHTS, SKILLS AND PROCEDURES YOU USED. SELECT FROM THE LIST BELOW

You wrote 64:

- ■ knowledge of the size of a chessboard
- ■ knowledge of squares, e.g. an 8 × 8 board will have 64 one-unit squares
- ■ counting
- ■ multiplication of single-digit numbers
- ■ square numbers

You wrote 92:

- ■ Select any from the above list and:
- ■ visualisation of the chessboard
- ■ visually divide the square into different-sized squares
- ■ select a strategy: elimination, systematically count . . .
- ■ addition

You wrote 204:

- ■ Select any from the above thoughts and:
- ■ accepting that different squares can overlap

You were unable to write a single number you felt confident in:

- ■ Select any from the above thoughts and:
- ■ knowledge that your mental checking procedures were not accurate
- ■ lacking confidence to do mental calculations without written confirmation
- ■ lacking confidence to do mental calculations without verbal confirmation
- ■ knowing that the answer 64 was too simple but not knowing what to do next
- ■ you have never attempted to solve a problem like this before.

at the end of the descriptions (see Table 5.7). This table summarises the qualities of each problem.

For the eight different problems, a selection of children's responses are provided combined with a brief analysis of the type of problem and, when appropriate, possible teaching approaches.

Problem 1: Number at Key Stage 1

I think of a number, then subtract 12. The answer is 26. What was my number? (DfEE 1999)

This is a one-step operation with only one solution.

An oral explanation may be the minimum required but a number sentence will show how this problem was solved.

Pupil responses:

'Count on from 26 up to the number'
'Add 12 and 26'

'Four more makes 30 and the eight left makes 38'
'26 take 12 makes 14'

The fourth response requires further 'word' analysis work.

Problem 2: Number at Key Stage 2

In a dance there are three boys and two girls in every line. Forty-two boys take part in the dance. How many girls take part? (DfEE 1999)

This is a multi-step operation with only one solution. An explanation of how the problem is solved may be recorded using numbers signs and symbols.

Pupil responses:

Jon gave an oral response of 'there are 14 groups of three boys making 42 altogether. The same number of groups for the girls means two fourteens. Which makes 28. Girls, 28 girls.'

The two examples below were written suggestions although the symbols used in the original child's work were little stick people!

$3 \times B = 42$
$B = 14$
$2 \times 14 = 28$ girls

or

BBBGG
BBBGG
BBBGG
. . .

repeated until there are 42 B symbols. The G symbols are totalled and the number 28 is written down.

Problem 3: Handshakes

There are twenty people in a room. Each person shakes hands once with every other person. How many handshakes will that be in total?

This problem could be called an investigation. It has one solution but the variety of methods leading to that solution may require the process of generalising. The explanation is considered almost more important than the final single number solution, the implication being that the explanation is the solution.

This type of problem requires a realisation by the child that a repeated diagram or calculation is possible but is not the most simple or 'elegant' method. The skills and procedures defined by Burton are applicable to this type of problem and may be used by a teacher to describe the approach and stages required by any child.

The problem is non-standard and therefore viewed by children when first introduced to it as a new problem requiring a new process for solution. The role of the teacher is crucial at the initial stage to ensure that the novelty of the problem does not become overwhelming and thus a threat to the child. The response 'can't do it' used to occur frequently in some classrooms. The teacher may reassure the children that the problem is well within their ability.

The 'handshakes' activity invites, almost begs for, a lively interactive demonstration of the problem itself at the start of the lesson. The confidence gained by every child, of all abilities, through a clear understanding of the problem itself may lead to an increased confidence in the mathematical approach to the solution. Teachers are not in total agreement over the preparation for such an investigation, but a practical example between a few children helps. The minimum mathematical skill required apart from understanding the way that numbers are written and ordered is addition. The ultimate, most 'elegant' process requires multiplication, proportion and interpretation of information in tables and diagrams, symbolisation and generalisation skills. Perhaps the most notable skill is the generalisation skill that once acquired will expand the child's repertoire of non-standard problems and hasten the problem's conclusion.

> At the start of the lesson the estimate of the answer to the problem elicits interesting responses from the children ranging from '20', '400', '100' and '180' to 'too many' and 'lots' (other responses do occur, often unpredictable, with good reasoning from the child). At this stage the teacher may consider the individual thought processes creating the different answers:
>
> '20' – this answer may indicate a total or partial misunderstanding of the problem itself;
>
> '400' – this answer indicates a child with a range of mathematical skills and an understanding of the problem itself, confident enough to make a reasonable conjecture;
>
> '100' – some mathematical skills shown here; child has confidence but probably using guessing skills rather than reasoning skills;
>
> '180' – either a sophisticated 'thinker' who has mathematical skills and has thought through several stages of the problem, or a good guess!
>
> 'lots' – this child may need more confidence during the early stages of solving the problem or may lack the mathematical skills to mentally consider three-digit numbers.

At the next stage of the lesson introducing the problem, the thinking and application of those thought process should be considered. Alternatively, a selection of the 'entry' and 'attack' procedures as described by Burton may be used. The problem is too complex to allow children to merely describe their processes orally; it is certainly worth 'modelling' a many-stages problem using oral answers only to exemplify the need for a written or diagrammatic record of each part of the process (for an example see Figure 5.2). A description of 'modelling' will include supporting children's own methods, not merely following another individual's procedure (Askew 1998).

The 'able' child's response

An able child may be able to provide a solution with no guidance and little written evidence once the rules of the problem have been restructured into a series of hypotheses and the logical deductions have been made.

> For example, James's response was 'Each of 20 people must shake hands with 19 others, as they cannot shake hands with themselves. That means 19 handshakes twenty times (i.e. 20 people shaking hands but not with themselves). But this will need to be halved as they cannot be double-counted, because TWO people only shake hands once.' The answer is 19 times 20 = 380 divided by 2 = 190.
>
> Daniel drew two parallel lines with 20 named or numbered 'people' on each line. The lines were joined by a mass of crossed lines representing each joining of hands!
>
> An able child will be able to explain the solution through adding the 19 starting handshakes to the next 18 then 17 then 16 down to 1 shake at the end: 19 + 18 + 17 + 16 + . . . + 3 + 2 + 1.

However, understanding the solution does not necessarily mean that the child will easily provide the proof or checking mechanism. Before this stage a generalisation may be attempted using the evidence within the solution. The idea that a general rule that works for a few probably works for all parts of the evidence provided within the same problem is not new to children studying mathematics at Key Stages 1 and 2.

Four people **A**li, **B**ob, **C**ate and **D**ave.

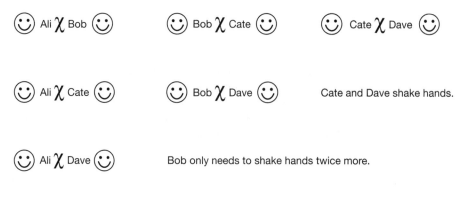

Ali shakes hands with Bob

Cate and Dave.

3 handshakes + 2 handshakes + 1 handshake = 6 handshakes in TOTAL

FIGURE 5.2 A diagrammatic explanation of the 'handshakes' problem between four people.

Even at Reception level the use of comparative words such as 'smaller' and 'bigger' is important for the development of problem-solving skills in which a general rule is found. The word 'more' may be considered a type of general rule itself.

The teacher may then create the cornerstone for future problem solving of the non-standard investigational type. At the next stage of problem solving an insight into the systematic approach may aid children's progress. This may be presented either as a reminder or as a taught process. The National Numeracy Strategy advocated 'estimate, calculate, check' and, when a problem is worked through, this sequence may be assumed to be taking place, although it should be noted that these three stages are not exactly equivalent to the three stages of problem solving described by Burton – 'entry, attack, review–extension' – although there are similarities.

Within the 'calculate' or 'attack' part of this approach to problem solving is contained the specialism that makes problem solving a unique aspect of mathematics or, as Cockcroft asserts, contains the heart of mathematics. The systematic aspect of problem solving is not essential to every problem but may enhance the rate of analysis and allows the child to develop methods for later use when more complex or mathematically demanding problems are presented. Many problems can be solved without such an approach but this is unlikely to provide a child with a strong framework for future problem solving for all types of problems.

The average child's response

Another beginning strategy may be to 'choose some simple cases'. Handshakes allows simple, small groups to be looked at and the number of handshakes counted. The written description may use diagrams or symbols but the data can be collated in a sequential format within a table (Table 5.5).

Generalising about rules and patterns appearing as the data is collected, testing those rules with previously collected or predicted data, possibly changing the generalisation or accepting it and ultimately using it to solve the problem – all this requires a relaxed 'playful' approach to the problem within a systematic approach.

The child who has chosen to draw the individuals shaking hands may choose about four or five people to start with (Figure 5.2). A child may recognise that the pattern of numbers recorded in the table is that of triangle numbers, thus recalling from memory a previously experienced pattern. This child may be able to predict the next and final solution using the knowledge of the pattern. Although this is not an essential part of primary development, the formula for h (the number of handshakes) expressed in terms of p (the number of people) is

$$h = 1/2p(p - 1)$$

TABLE 5.5 Representation of results in a table

NUMBER OF PEOPLE	NUMBER OF HANDSHAKES
1	0
2	1
3	3
4	6

Problem 4: Lost pet

> Lucy has lost her cat. The cat is the same age as Lucy and usually follows her half-way to school. When Lucy returned home after school the cat was not waiting for food in the usual place. How should Lucy find her pet?

This problem is again a 'real-world' problem with varied solutions and varied methods. Is this a mathematical problem? Should this type of problem be considered in the same curriculum area as numeracy? The answers to these questions are debatable and the decision to use any problem in the classroom rests with the individual preferences of the teacher.

The skills required for problem solving remain the same and many of the processes are the same. It is a problem involving time, distance, shape and space, maps, memory, visualising and an extremely systematic approach. Depending on the method decided upon to solve this problem, even collecting data and writing questionnaires will raise the solution to a high level of expertise.

The problem is specific but has no one solution and the variety of solutions and their preceding methods provide avenues into other curriculum areas. The key process involved here is making assumptions. If the investigators decide that the cat went home after the walk half-way to school this is an assumption as there is no evidence for this until data have been collected through questionnaires, for example. The assumption keeps the problem focused on one place, home. This may prove beneficial to the teacher and allow practice in non-numerical mental skills and using correct vocabulary when children are memorising a route through their house.

Problem 5a: Arithmogon

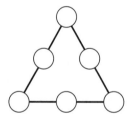

Put 1, 2 or 3 in each circle so each side adds up to five.

Problem 5b: Miranda's Morning Maths

> This problem is a variation on the oral and mental starter, called here 'Miranda's Morning Maths', based on the television programme *Countdown*. The children may choose any operation or combination of operations to find the answers provided. The solution in this activity is the chosen procedure as both starting point and finishing point are given. If 2, 3, 5 and 10 are the start numbers and the answers are 25, 50, 15, 20 and 250, any correct mathematical operations may be accepted using only

the start numbers listed. The teacher requires the children to practise operations with multiples of 5 and 10 in this case. A type of activity allowing children to view the variety of correct but different approaches may be a valuable part of problem-solving training. For example, which is the correct method out of

$(2 + 3) \times 5 = 25$ and $(5 \times 10) \div 2 = 25$?

These two types of problem have a variety of solutions; occasionally the apparently different solutions are the same – in the case of arithmogons possible rotations of each other – rather than actual numerically different solutions. The use of puzzles using a repeated 'skeleton' or 'form' is important for the apparent familiarity of the problem. Children can feel confident that they have successfully met a similar type before, thus allowing the teacher to manipulate the complexity of the task. The teacher can differentiate for ability or even skill areas: fractions or decimals as a change from whole numbers, multiplication instead of subtraction. A repeated skeleton for the problem also allows children to try out their own problem-writing talents.

Problem 6: Redesign your bedroom (Koshy 2001)

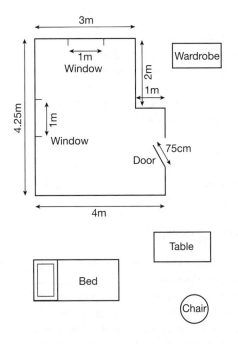

Your parents have offered to redesign your bedroom now that you have grown out of the small bed used when you were young. They have given you a limit of £600 and an Argos catalogue. Choose the furniture that you need in your bedroom. A plan of your bedroom is provided. Place the furniture in the correct place in your bedroom.

A similar problem is used by Casey and Koshy (2001) with 7- and 8-year-olds.

This is a standard or 'real-life' problem with many solutions but a limited number of methods. Each child may collect, classify, sort and interpret data; money and measuring calculations are required and drawing skills for representing the solution are essential.

The approach used is systematic and testing; analysing and eliminating are parts of the main problem-solving process incorporating estimating and checking throughout the activity.

Problem 7: Frogs

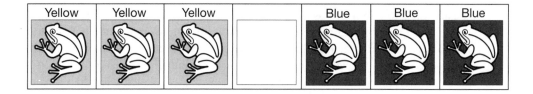

What is the minimum number of moves required to change the positions of the frogs so that the yellow frogs move to the lily pads occupied by the blue frogs and the blue frogs move to the lily pads occupied by the yellow frogs? There is one blank lily pad in the middle. The frogs can only move in a particular way:

each frog can only move in one direction;
each frog can slide into an empty space;
each frog can jump over a frog of a different colour.

The software for this problem and a simpler version called Tadpoles is available through SMILE mathematics (SMILE 2001).

This is a puzzle and is non-standard and there is only one final numerical solution to the problem as it is phrased above. In a similar manner to the handshakes problem, the use of generalisation to prove the minimum number of moves is not necessary for finding the single solution.

Using the context of a problem

The main difference between the solution to the frogs problem and the solution to the handshakes problem is that the context of the frogs problem provides extension material and challenging problems for the most able children in the class.

The handshakes problem has a context that allows limited development, as people have only two hands and increasing numbers or introducing proportional numbers of people greeting each other is the limit of the extension, unless aliens with unusual appendages are introduced!

The frogs problem allows changes in the rules, the number of frogs on each side, the number of spaces and the number of different colours, and an extra dimension could be introduced for exceptionally ambitious children – all within the same context but each time asking 'What if . . . ?'

The minimum number of moves for the puzzle described above is fifteen.

Problem 8: Chessboard

How many squares are there on a chessboard?

This is a puzzle that requires an understanding of the nature of the question. At face value an understanding of the size of the board and possibly the game of chess may be necessary. However, once the answer sixty-four has been suggested as incomplete, a systematic process of analysis is required. This problem, apparently simple to answer, relying on memory and specific knowledge, is an investigation of a similar type to that of the handshakes investigation. There is only one solution and, for the context defined in the question, it allows little extension. Once the child realises that different sizes of squares may be considered, calculations including diagrams, tabular representation of the data and multiplication and addition skills – even some understanding of square numbers – may be used. The single solution to the problem set is:

$$(8 \times 8) + (7 \times 7) + (6 \times 6) + (5 \times 5) + (4 \times 4) + (3 \times 3) + (2 \times 2) + (1 \times 1)$$

Diagrams will help the understanding of this question greatly, for example Figure 5.3 illustrates one type of diagram to help solve the 'chessboard' problem.

Recent developments and functional mathematics

The approaches described in the following paragraphs are largely based on a mathematics enrichment project designed for 11-year-old students by a team at Brunel University during the years 2008–2010.

The work includes description of the materials used, the mathematical skills required to complete any tasks and details of teacher–pupil communication with an emphasis on self-tracking.

The problems themselves can be regarded as routine practice exercises or more complex tasks requiring some degree of metacognition. It is the difficulty or complexity that makes them (the problems) genuinely problematic, a statement obvious to many but explained in detail in research from Queensland, Australia (Galbraith and Renshaw 2000). The study indicates seven levels of difficulty to be mastered and it is the subsequent lack of progression towards solving the problem that may cause the solver to not find a solution or even misunderstand totally.

To facilitate the ease of solving of a particular problem, video clips of 'real-life' situations taken from YouTube give students instant focus and more immediate understanding. When told at the start of the video clip that questions will be asked about the content, over 80 per cent of children recognised appropriate mathematical vocabulary within the clip accurately.

One challenge was to make a musical instrument that played three distinct notes (see Figure 5.4). Materials provided were paper, card, used sweet containers and a mouthpiece from a recorder. Try this activity yourself; it is great fun and very difficult to accomplish accurately. The skills used are mainly measuring and geometry; understanding of the problem is gained from the video clip of recorders being made, and analysis, exploration, planning and implementation are mostly practical and use

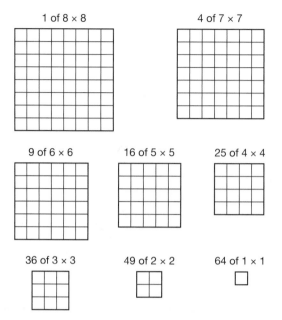

1 of 8 × 8

4 of 7 × 7

9 of 6 × 6

16 of 5 × 5

25 of 4 × 4

36 of 3 × 3

49 of 2 × 2

64 of 1 × 1

FIGURE 5.3 A diagram to help solve the 'chessboard' problem.

functional mathematics. It is worth noting that the most successful group of children in this activity did not follow the normal recorder design.

The 'handshakes' problem can be redesigned into the 'Do-si-do' problem. The context has now become a choreographic one. Children discuss and then try out physically and some even use mental skills to predict solutions. I strongly recommend practising your do-si-do demonstration before starting the lesson.

Activity: Do-si-do

Outside; in pairs, 'do-si-do' with your partner.

Join with another pair. How many 'do-si-dos' would you need to do so that you have changed places with everyone in your group once?

Each group of four join with another group of four. How many 'do-si-dos' are needed to dance with everyone *once*?

Now think about how to find out how many 'do-si-dos' you might need for the whole group (fifty people). You need diagrams and a method of recording to help you.

Note: Do-si-do is a back-to-back exchange of places with your opposite partner.

Return inside to try to find a way to work out the solution for any number of people. This mathematics can be used for dancing in groups and choreography.

Strategy knowledge may be taught but understanding how to apply the newly learnt strategy can be guided by the teacher using 'modelling', questioning and even demonstration including dancing.

Responses

Children are encouraged to record all findings, ideas and calculations used to solve a problem and the teacher can guide this process by creating an appropriate response sheet. The evidence suggests that 'response tables' with starting numbers aid development of different systematic recording techniques. Sequential tabulation, diagrams and graphical representation can provide student guidance even before any numerical calculation is performed.

How the teacher uses any response is crucial, whether it is analysing the directed response provided in the table or selecting material from question and answer sessions. How do *you* reply to the child who asks 'Why are we doing this?' or 'How will this help me later on?' It is useful to prepare two or three responses that satisfy the children's curiosity.

Using a reflective journal

A journal recording a child's progress of understanding, particularly in relation to previous work, reveals consolidation that can be referred to at a much later date.

Before teaching your next mathematics class try completing the journal guidance

Making SWEET Music

Name: ....

My group made .... different notes	
We used .... to make the instrument	
The instrument: Length Circumference Diameter Radius Surface area Distance between holes Draw an accurate scale drawing on the back of this	

FIGURE 5.4 A musical instrument activity.

as though you are one of the children you teach and compare your responses with an actual child's responses. There may be some surprising results. When 11-year-old children, following an intervention project at Brunel University, completed a journal after every session teachers noticed a startling improvement in the appropriate use of mathematical vocabulary and in understanding the role of the journal in their learning (see Table 5.6).

Journal guidance

This is what we did:

This is what I learnt:

How does this connect with something in everyday life?

What are you still not sure about?

This is the maths I used:

How does this connect with something you have done before at school?

What would you like to know more about?

A summary of the eight problems

For each of the eight problems presented in this chapter Table 5.7 summarises the problem, type of activity and mathematical skill used, possible processes used during the solution and appropriate learning objectives. Further explanation of the words describing the processes can be found at the end of the chapter.

Throughout the short descriptions of skills and processes involved in approaching different types of problems, two essential skills have not been mentioned. First, I will add a section on the role of information and communication technology (ICT) in problem solving, looking at two very different approaches currently practised in this country. Second, I will include a brief section mentioning the importance of mental skills, more details of which can be found in Chapter 3.

Information and communication technology

Calculators are not advocated as essential for problem solving. The nature of the skills involved is unlikely to need support from calculators. An exception would be when the energies of the child are required for the strategy rather than the calculation.

Tony Gardiner, who has coordinated the UK Mathematical Challenges at secondary school level (ages 11–15 years) for several years, insists that all of the problems set

TABLE 5.6 Response to journal question 'What would you like to know more about?'

DATE	MATHS-SPECIFIC STATEMENT	GENERAL STATEMENT	NO RESPONSE
June	54%	21%	25%
December	75%	12.5%	12.5%

TABLE 5.7 A summary of the eight problems

PROBLEM ACTIVITY	TYPES OF ACTIVITY	MATHEMATICAL SKILLS	PROCESS	LEARNING OBJECTIVES FROM FRAMEWORK
1. Number at Key Stage 1	Standard word problem *One solution* *Limited methods*	Addition, subtraction, commutative law	Classifying Undoing Testing	Solving simple word problems set in 'real-life' contexts and explaining how the problem was solved
2. Number at Key Stage 2	Standard word problem *One solution* *One method*	Addition, subtraction, fractions, ratio, proportion	Classifying Combining Making rules Symbolising Testing	Using all four operations to solve word problems involving numbers in 'real life'
3. Handshakes	Non-standard 'word' problem *One solution* *Varied methods*	Visualising, kinaesthetic demonstration, addition, multiplication	Conjecturing Making rules Generalising Changing rules Symbolising Testing Proving	Organising and using data Making decisions Reasoning or generalising about numbers or shapes Identifying and using appropriate operations
4. Lost pet	'Real-word' problem *Varied solution* *Varied methods*	Memorising facts, number, distance, time. Visual representation	Guessing Systematising Hypothesising Reasoning from assumptions	Reasoning and generalising Identifying and using appropriate operations involving quantities Explaining methods and reasoning
5. Arithmogon	Puzzle *Limited solutions* *Varied methods*	Four operations and their inverses, commutative law	Classifying Testing Making rules	Choosing and using appropriate number operations to solve problems
6. Bedroom problem for £600	Standard problem of 'real life' *Many solutions* *Varied methods*	Visualisation. Addition, subtraction, area, money calculations	Making rules Changing rules Demonstrating Testing Interpreting diagrams	Reasoning or generalising about shapes Using all four operations to solve money problems

TABLE 5.7 continued

PROBLEM ACTIVITY	TYPES OF ACTIVITY	MATHEMATICAL SKILLS	PROCESS	LEARNING OBJECTIVES FROM FRAMEWORK
7. Frogs	Puzzle, non-standard *One solution* *Varied methods*	Kinaesthetic interpretation, visualisation, four operations, representative diagrams	Making rules Symbolising Hypothesising Testing Proving Generalising	Solving mathematical problems Explaining and recognising patterns and relationships Using a symbol to stand for an unknown Generalising and predicting Extend by asking 'What if . . . ?'
8. Chessboard	Puzzle *One solution* *Varied methods*	Memorising facts, addition, multiplication, visualisation	Classifying Conjecturing Justifying Testing Ordering Interpreting diagrams	Recognising patterns Using an appropriate number operation and method of calculating

in the challenges are done without a calculator. He believes that good problems make children think, and then learn from their mistakes (Gardiner 1996).

The onus is therefore on the problem setter or the teacher to provide the appropriate problem. He also adapts the usual school textbook language, thus encouraging children to develop the skill of making mathematical sense of simple problems without the clues usually present in the 'familiar, predictable, highly suggestive language'. The techniques are standard one-step routine questions with multiple-choice answers but each problem needs to be understood, interpreted and quickly responded to. Some questions ask for more than one step in their solution and a routine method will not be appropriate in many cases. The 'setting' of a problem may include an element of surprise and above all the questions are designed to be fun. The inappropriateness of calculators in a mathematics classroom is summarised by Gardiner in the statement that mathematics is a mental universe. This is a view held by many mathematicians but I have found that ICT used appropriately can be an aid to mathematical concept development rather than a hindrance. The problems within the UK challenges are designed for the more able 35 per cent of the population. The role of ICT for these problems is to allow exploration of a wider range of tasks than is possible with just pencil and paper.

The developments of computer use and more widespread internet access have allowed teachers to use a greater range of methods of communication with the children they teach. Teachers have created online 'blogs' to allow children time to share answers and solutions directly and immediately whilst completing homework tasks.

Role of mental arithmetic

My classroom observations reveal mental arithmetic as crucial to any solving method. Without access to numerical mental skills, the problem solver may be severely hindered. Certain types of problems allow mental skills to be used but other types require mental arithmetic skills, for example an arithmogon solution may indicate other skills than problem solving if written methods or calculators are used. A comprehensive knowledge of number bonds and facts about the four operations will speed up any process during part of the solution to a problem.

So can problem solving be taught?

The National Numeracy Strategy, used in primary schools for some time and introduced in all secondary schools at Key Stage 3 in September 2001, advocates problem solving as an integral part of standard lessons – both the application of mathematics to everyday situations within the child's experience and the great deal of discussion and oral work before the written form (DfEE 2001). So there is an expectation that problem solving will be taught using the approaches set out in the frameworks of the National Numeracy Strategy and the National Curriculum.

Evidence within this writing indicates that mathematical skills can be taught and the processes can be demonstrated, explained and experienced within the mathematics classroom. However, a child may not 'learn' how to solve a problem unless he or she experiences a problem, and then perceives that he or she has solved that problem effectively. Once a child has created his or her 'own' model to use when presented with another problem, the approach may be developed using taught mathematical skills and trained processes. Children with the opportunity to share approaches to problem solving with each other will be exposed to an even greater number of models and potential learning situations.

Once the child produces an oral or written response to a problem the teacher may start a record of the skills and process used by that child. This teacher record would be in addition to any record or self-evaluation that the child records, including a journal. The monitoring and assessment of progress resulting from the training in problem solving that the individual child receives may naturally evolve from the type and frequency of problems set. Types of assessment are discussed in Chapter 8.

Summary

In this chapter I have attempted to explain some concepts of problem solving. First, the establishment of problem solving as an integral part of the school curriculum, both in primary school and secondary school, was accepted and found to contain similarities across all Key Stages and many other curriculum areas of study. Upon examination of types of problems and different words used to describe the approaches to solving problems, inconsistencies were found. Most of the inconsistencies relate to descriptions of strategies used when analysing the method of problem solving. To clarify these inconsistencies I suggest that mathematical skills, both written and mental, can be taught and applied when solving a problem. The child may have the skills available to use during the process of solving the problem. The process is the aspect of solving a problem that requires training: training through repetition, discussion with peers, variety of context and enjoyment of the challenge itself. ICT and mental arithmetic skills are relevant to the process and usually are used to enhance the process in some manner. The process may become faster if mental calculations occur rather than pen and paper ones, and a calculator or computer may be used to challenge the more able children and aid focus on the process instead of the calculation.

An emphasis on functional mathematics and 'real' situations will make the problem relevant to a child, thus increasing the motivation to solve any problem completely. Using a self-tracking journal appears to develop vocabulary and understanding of the role of reflection following the problem-solving process.

I have used eight problems of very different types to create some direction and application to the approaches to problem solving and provide easier access to some key problem-solving words and vocabulary. All eight problems have been used effectively in the classroom and may provide you with some guidance or ideas for future lessons.

Dictionary of terms used in the 'process' of problem solving

Assumption Something accepted as true or certain to happen without proof.

Classifying Arranging information in categories according to shared qualities or characteristics.

Combining Joining of different qualities in such a way that their individual distinctiveness is retained.

Conjecturing Conclusion formed on the basis of incomplete information.

Changing rules Altering one or more starting principles.

Demonstrating Clearly showing the existence or truth by giving evidence.

Generalising Making general or broad statements.

Guessing Estimating without sufficient information to be sure of being correct.

Hypothesis A supposition or proposed explanation made on the basis of limited evidence as a starting point for further investigation.

Hypothesising Putting something forward as a hypothesis.

Interpret diagrams Explain the meaning of, or evidence shown by, a drawing, graph, table or statistical representation.

Making rules Creating the principles or guidelines for an activity or strategy.

Ordering Arranging things in relation to each other according to a particular sequence, pattern or method.

Proving Testing the accuracy of a mathematical calculation through demonstrating using evidence or argument.

Reasoning from assumptions Find an answer to a problem using assumptions.

Symbolising Using symbols to represent or stand for something else.

System An organised scheme or method, using a set of rules.

Systematising Arranging according to an organised system.

Testing Taking measures to check the quality or reliability of something.

Undoing Reversing the effects/results of a previous calculation or measure.

References

Askew, M. (1998) *Teaching Primary Mathematics*. London: Hodder and Stoughton.

Askew, M. and Wiliam, D. (1995) *Recent Research in Mathematics Education 5–16*. London: Ofsted.

Burton, L. (1986) *Thinking Things Through*. Oxford: Blackwell.

Casey, R. and Koshy, V. (2001) *Bright Challenges*. London: The Elephas Centre.

Cockcroft, W. H. (1982) *Mathematics Counts. Report of the Committee of Inquiry into the Teaching of Mathematics in Schools*. London: HMSO.

DfEE (1999) *The Framework for Teaching Mathematics from Reception to Year 6*. London: Department for Education and Employment.

DfEE (2001) *The Framework for Teaching Mathematics: Years 7, 8 and 9*. London: Department for Education and Employment.

DfEE/QCA (1999) *The National Curriculum for England*. London: Department for Education and Employment and Qualifications and Curriculum Authority.

Gardiner, A. (1996) *Mathematical Challenges*. Cambridge: Cambridge University Press.

Galbraith, G. and Renshaw, P. (2000) 'A source of insight into problem solving', *CIMT International Journal for Mathematics Teaching and Learning*, 3: 80.

Kent, D. (ed.) (1996) *London GCSE Mathematics*. Oxford: Heinemann.

Koshy, V. (2001) *Teaching Mathematics to Able Children*. London: David Fulton.

Pearsall, J. (ed.) (2001) *The New Oxford Dictionary of English*. Oxford: Oxford University Press.

QCDA (2010) http://www.qcda.gov.uk

SMILE (2001) *MicroSMILE Mathematical Puzzles*. London: SMILE Mathematics.

Useful websites

http://www.spartacus.schoolnet.co.uk

http://www.cylex-uk.co.uk

http://nrich.maths.org

http://www.m-a.org.uk

http://www.qcda.gov.uk

http://www.atm.org.uk

http://nationalstrategies.standards.dcsf.gov.uk/primary/primaryframework/mathematics/

Numeracy and low attaining children

Jean Murray, with Caroline Clissold

Introduction

Concern about children who struggle to learn mathematics has been high on the national mathematics education agenda for many years. As the Williams Report (Williams 2008) spells out, this concern is part of the current initiative to raise standards in schooling and reflects ongoing analyses of the mathematical performance of children in the UK in relation to pupils of similar age in other countries [see the Programme for International Assessment (PISA) and the Trends in International Mathematics and Science Study (TIMMS)]. Low attainment in mathematics is also a vital issue because children who struggle with the subject may reach the end of their compulsory schooling without gaining the functional knowledge of mathematics that will enable them to participate confidently in adult life.

In this chapter children who struggle with mathematics are called 'low attainers', drawing on the definition of this term used by Derek Haylock (1991). Haylock rejects a variety of labels for children who struggle with mathematics, including 'less able children', 'slow learners' and 'underachievers', because of their connotations of negativity. He opts for the term 'low attainers' to describe children 'who need special help and provision in mathematics' and whose progress in the subject is a cause for concern (p. 10). These are the children who would be in the bottom 25 per cent of ' a notional ability range for their peer group' (p. 10). The reasons for such patterns of low attainment in mathematics are 'varied, complex, idiosyncratic and unpredictable' (p. 9). Such a definition inevitably involves some norm-referenced judgements in that low attaining children are 'assessed' in relation to their more able peers. But this should not obscure the all-important fact that the majority of these children are also underachieving in relation to their *own* potential in mathematics. And the key focus in 'unlocking' mathematics for low attaining children is that any initiatives to help them should, as a fundamental starting point, further the development of this individual potential.

There is a raft of current national initiatives designed to address the needs of children who find mathematics challenging. These include the guidance called 'Overcoming Barriers in Mathematics', the 'Springboard' initiatives, the 'Wave 3' materials, the availability of one-to-one tuition programmes for eligible children in

Years 5 and 6 and the developing 'Numbers Count' programme for Key Stage 1 children. Most of these initiatives are designed to support and develop children at one level below the national average for their ages as determined by teacher assessment or tests at Key Stage 1 (Year 2, age 7) and Key Stage 2 (Year 6, age 11).

Many of these initiatives have considerable strengths. The 'Overcoming Barriers' guidance, for example, focuses on one mathematical objective for which it provides a teaching programme and detailed teaching guidance and a useful follow-up assessment schedule. Many schools have reported that the one-to-one tuition programmes in Years 5 and 6 have boosted the confidence and competence of the low attaining children attending these classes. The provision is also reported to have enabled these children to become more mathematically proficient and to achieve higher scores in the end of Key Stage 2 national tests.

There is then clearly much of value in the various national initiatives, but most are in essence 'catch up' programmes, which aim to address particular areas of perceived weakness or deficit in mathematics (often only in number) and thereby to enable the target children to gain more benefit from the main teaching programme for their year group. These aims reflect the national concern with raising children's mathematical achievement, particularly in relation to the end of Key Stage 2 tests. Worthy and well-intentioned as such initiatives may be, support for low attainers should not just be short term to facilitate passing a test; nor should it just be about raising attainment in relation to the peer group for the sake of school or national targets. Rather support should be about creating the foundations for long-term, ongoing patterns of attainment in mathematics for each and every individual child and his or her future as a numerate member of society.

This chapter looks at the knowledge and understanding of addition and subtraction, as used in mental calculations, of a group of mathematically low attaining children. The findings show that these 9- and 10-year-olds could be divided into three groups according to the calculation methods they used. The learning components of mathematics can be considered as facts, skills, concepts (including understanding of deep conceptual structures such as place value, which underpin our number system), strategies and attitudes. The chapter argues that in order to achieve long-term patterns of success in the subject it is crucial that children's *confidence* and *competence* in numeracy are both raised. In other words children need both the knowledge and the understanding of the relevant facts, skills, concepts and strategies ('competence' is used here as a convenient, if somewhat limited, shorthand term for this complex network of mathematical knowledge and learning), and the *confidence* in their own ability to use and apply these things successfully.

Low attaining children and mental calculations

The case studies reported in this chapter focus on low attaining children in the middle of Year 5 of their primary schooling. All the children were aged between 9 and 10 years of age at the time of the assessment and came from a large primary school in a socially mixed and ethnically diverse area of a large city. The school follows the national guidance for mathematics teaching. At the time of the research these Year 5 children had had four and a half years of teaching that followed this national guidance for Key Stage 1 and 2 mathematics. Their numeracy work had therefore included a heavy emphasis on mental calculations. In addition to the assessments detailed below, the case study data collected also included individual mathematical records back to earlier years of schooling.

The focus group was chosen using Haylock's definition of low attainers, given above, as a guide to ensure selection of an appropriate sample. Each child was assessed using a basic assessment schedule devised to find out:

- addition and subtractions that she or he knew by heart (as 'instant recall' knowledge);

- addition and subtraction calculations that she or he could work out using relevant calculation strategies ('quick' recall);

- the strategies that she or he used for 'quick' recall calculations.

The calculations were presented to the children orally and in a horizontal, written layout. The emphasis of the assessment was on using mental calculation methods throughout, although in order to ensure continuity with the national guidance the children were encouraged to use written jottings to assist with the mental calculations, as and when needed. The children had no access to resources such as ready-made number lines, number squares or other support materials.

Analysis of the assessment findings showed that the children could be split into three groups, according to their calculation methods. These groups were named *continuing counters*, *beginning strategists* and *algorithm clingers*. In the following sections of this chapter the key characteristics of each group are briefly described. Case studies of individual children then extend and exemplify these characteristics.

Continuing counters

Children in this group tackled nearly all the sums by counting on one-by-one. Some children just counted orally, either out loud or in subdued mutterings; others accompanied their oral counting with finger counting, nods of the head or attempts to trace lines on the desktop as they counted. These movements were obvious attempts to 'tally' or keep track of the oral counting.

Jodie-Anne was typical of children in this group in that she counted on or back on her fingers to obtain the answer to nearly all the sums, tackling each sum just as it was presented to her. Often seeming panicked by the questions, she did not check her answers or respond to prompts to try to find an alternative calculation method. She also clearly struggled to understand some key mathematical vocabulary such as 'partitioning' and 'multiple' and was reluctant to talk about her mathematics. With calculations involving small numbers Jodie-Anne often achieved accurate answers with her finger counting; with larger numbers, not surprisingly, she frequently miscounted and appeared to have little 'feel for numbers' (e.g. estimation skills) to help her judge whether or not her answer was correct, as the extract below indicates:

Teacher: 'What is 37 + 8?'

Jodie-Anne: '48, no, wait, don't know if that's right, no, 85.'

Teacher: 'How did you get that answer?'

Jodie-Anne: 'I thinked [sic] about it and then counted on 8 with my fingers.'

Counting on one-by-one was then an unreliable strategy for Jodie-Anne, but she had little sense of drawing on other calculation methods or of using the factual knowledge of some addition and subtraction bonds and number order that she did have (e.g. in line with one of the current Year 2 objectives she could, with reasonable speed, say the number that was one more or one less than a stated number and give the number that was ten more or ten less than a multiple of 10). Prompted to explore if she could use this kind of knowledge for calculation, she consistently replied 'don't know'. At only one point in the assessment did she vary her strategy, showing some evidence of counting on in twenties rather than in ones, an indication of an embryonic, sound mental calculation strategy. Perhaps not surprisingly, her knowledge of two-digit place value (numbers 0–100) was generally insecure, particularly her knowledge of how to partition numbers into ones and tens.

Young children begin counting groups of objects by counting one-by-one, so, for example, many 5-year-olds would calculate 4 + 3 by counting 1, 2, 3, 4 (to check that the four objects really are four) and then counting on 3 (or three 'single units') by counting 5, 6, 7. In the early years of numeracy, then, a 'unit' is a single and whole entity and so counting a group of objects or calculating a simple sum involves 'seeing' each object or number as a separate and single 'unit' and using a one-by-one count (often accompanied by touching objects or using fingers to 'tally' or check the count). Progressing on from this stage, children then begin to start their count from the 4 (i.e. not needing to check that four is four) but still adding on the 3 using one-by-one counting. However, still later growth in understanding of number is marked by a fundamental change in what is considered as a 'unit', so children progress on to understanding that a 'unit' may also be a group of objects (or a 'composite unit'). This idea of the 'composite unit' is fundamental to children's understanding of place value (in which a 10, then a 100, 1000 etc. become the 'unit' for calculation); once acquired, understanding of the composite unit can also be used in calculations as the basis of various 'shortcut' strategies. So in adding 4 + 3, children can eventually progress to treating the '4' as a 'composite unit' to add to a second such 'composite unit' of '3'. Continuing counters in this research appeared to have either not acquired or not implemented this understanding of the composite unit in their calculation methods.

Counting one-by-one and 'tagging' objects or using fingers for keeping track of the count (ensuring that one number counted corresponds to one object and that each number is counted once and only once) remains a useful and, in some contexts, effective counting strategy into adult life (e.g. an adult may use this strategy to check or double check how many people are due to visit for a meal or when putting out the correct number of chairs for those visitors). However, as Jodie-Anne's case illustrates it is not a reliable or rapid strategy for calculations with large numbers.

Unfortunately, reliance on the strategy of counting on in ones, in inappropriate contexts such as large calculations, by low attaining children can be common, even in the latter stages of Key Stage 2. Counting in this way appears to provide a kind of 'mathematical security blanket' for children who, for a variety of reasons, have not developed or chosen to implement a wider range of knowledge and strategies. Success in achieving the right answer with *some* calculations involving small numbers encourages them to continue using this basic counting method, when they need to move on to develop instant recall knowledge of number bonds and a wider range of calculation strategies. Over-reliance on this basic strategy may mask children's difficulties in remembering number facts, another factor that is associated with low attainers (Bird 2007; Houssart 2004). Alternatively, it may be that overdependence on one-by-one counting removes the need to learn addition bonds, which in turn limits the development of children's strategic methods.

Beginning strategists

This group showed evidence of a range of developing strategies, used alongside some factual knowledge of number bonds. Damien was a typical 'beginning strategist' as in his assessment he showed some developing strengths in his knowledge and understanding of mental calculations. He had a sound knowledge of number bonds and number order to 100 and some embryonic strategies. He knew – and answered quickly – the questions about number order, saying that he 'just knew' the answers. For other simple addition and subtraction bonds he gave the answer and stated that 'I just know it'.

Asked to work out 48 + 50 he answered correctly and quickly and then explained his strategy as 'I know my 20s so added 40 (*as 20 and then another 20*) on to 50 then added 8'. Adding 38 to 20 he also worked correctly, 'knowing' that 30 and 20 is 50 'same as before'. His strategy of counting in multiples of 10 or 20 was then effective for these sums. However, when he was asked to calculate the answers in another way, it became clear that this was his one and only calculation strategy for this type of addition sum.

Damien's strategies for subtraction were also beginning to develop, although he found it very hard to articulate these. For example, asked to explain how he calculated 72 – 14, he said he 'leaves' the 72, 'memorises' it and takes away 14 (exactly how is not clear from the transcript), but this strategy did enable him to achieve the correct answer.

These useful strategies, however, were interspersed with other ad hoc and not always reliable strategies, particularly for subtraction, as the following extract shows:

> Teacher: 'What's 49 – 27?' (*long silence follows*)
> Damien: 'Is it 16?'
> Teacher: 'Not quite.'
> Damien: 'Actually I got 15.'
> Teacher: 'How did you get that?'
> Damien: 'First I thought it was an add, then I saw the symbol [sic] so I took 20 from 40, then added 9 and 7 and then took that away from 20.'

The strategy that Damien is using here, and the conceptual understanding of the inverse relationship between addition and subtraction that may be underpinning it, clearly need further exploration through teacher assessment. However, this could be a challenging task, given Damien's hesitance in talking about his mathematics.

With other calculations involving two-digit numbers, Damien openly resorted to guess work or one-by-one counting in order to supply answers and showed a *laissez-faire* attitude to whether or not the answer was correct. Intriguingly he seemed to find it difficult to use and apply his sound understanding of number order between 0 and 100 and multiples of 10 in solving these mental calculations.

Typically, beginning strategists as a group had one favoured strategy for a particular type and size of calculation (with addition calculations involving two two-digit numbers Damien, for example, consistently said that he 'used his 20s' to partition one of the numbers). Partitioning into 10s and 20s was a common strategy across this group. Other favoured strategies for addition were doubling and use of near doubles, rounding up or down and adding on from the largest number. For subtraction, strategies such as counting up from the smaller number to the larger in order to find the difference between the two was a favoured strategy for dealing with calculations such as 56 – 47. These strategies formed the starting points for a good repertoire of calculation methods from which the children might have been able to select the most appropriate method for the particular calculation context. However, most beginning strategists stuck to one, or at most two, favoured strategies, regardless of the nature or size of the sum, and showed little confidence in seeking or trying out alternative ways of calculating the answer.

Most of the children showed a sound knowledge of two-digit place value, but the assessment indicated that some of them, like Damien in the subtraction example above, might have limited conceptual understanding of the inverse relationship between addition and subtraction. Further assessments would be needed to test such understanding, but if such conceptual knowledge was not secure then that would inhibit the ability to implement a range of strategies consistently, confidently and accurately.

Limited or insecure conceptual knowledge might also indicate that some beginning strategists had restricted starting points from which to generate new knowledge. A previous study (Murray 1999: 165) of children's mental calculations showed how an able child, with the support of careful teacher questioning, was able to use her conceptual understanding of number as a mathematical springboard for the creation of new knowledge. However, there were no indications in this current research study that beginning strategists had the confidence to forge new knowledge in this way. Looking ahead in their mathematical learning journeys, the danger might then be that they become stuck with limited ways of working, rather than expanding their repertoires of strategies, underpinned by sound mathematical knowledge and understanding.

Algorithm clingers

Despite the emphasis on using mental calculations in the assessment, the third group, named *algorithm clingers*, tackled nearly all the questions by using a written sum (an arithmetical algorithm, which, as Exercise 14 in Chapter 1 explains, is a procedure for calculation). Most of the children used 'standard' written algorithms, that is, sums that are commonly used and taught, as their preferred way to solve the calculations they were asked to tackle.

Leah was a typical algorithm clinger. Her records showed a pattern of under-achievement in mathematics going back to Key Stage 1. They also indicated that she had often been very anxious about her number work, particularly about 'getting sums wrong'. She also struggled with using and applying mathematical language, although she had good knowledge of addition and subtraction number bonds using numbers 0–20. Leah's parents had tried to ease her anxiety by sending her to out-of-school-hours numeracy classes, which implemented a systematic programme of rote learning about how to 'do' standard written algorithms. Ideally this new set of skills should have provided her with a valuable confidence boost, a quick fix 'solution' for her mathematical problems and anxieties. Certainly by clinging on to her knowledge of how to 'do' these algorithms she could answer some of the sums in the pedestrian mathematics scheme that the out-of-school classes used. However, in school, where a variety of mental calculation strategies and both standard and non-standard written algorithms were in use, Leah's achievement pattern was far more variable. She then became even more anxious and demoralised and her progress slowed to a snail's pace.

Asked to tackle the sum 37 + 8, Leah immediately picked up a pencil and wrote down an algorithm:

$$\begin{array}{r} 37 \\ \underline{8+} \\ 45 \end{array}$$

She laboriously added up the units column and then the tens before proudly giving her correct answer. Asked if she knew another way of calculating the answer, Leah said a simple 'no'; prompted to consider what number facts or mental strategies she might be able to use to help her to work out the answer, she replied 'I don't know'. In this case the written algorithm brought Leah success in the form of a correct answer, but it also appeared to paralyse her in terms of generating other strategies or of drawing on her knowledge of number facts for a calculation that should have been easy to answer using mental methods.

Leah also used a written algorithm for subtraction questions. In the case below she seemed to be attempting to use the standard written decomposition algorithm for subtraction (see Exercise 16 in Chapter 1) to solve the problem:

$$\begin{array}{r} 72 \\ 14- \end{array}$$

She worked this sum out by starting in the units column and subtracting the 2 from the 4; she then moved on to the tens column and subtracted 1 from 7. For Leah, the standard written algorithm for subtraction using the decomposition method (see Exercise 14 in Chapter 1 for further information) has gone wrong here: following the rules she has been taught she has started by working the units column, but then seems to have 'forgotten' how this algorithm operates and has made a classic children's error in operating this kind of sum called 'take the smaller number from the larger number regardless' (see Hansen 2005).

Learning how to 'do' standard written algorithms, then, gave algorithm clingers a limited repertoire of skills in written mathematics which they could operate, usually competently, if the sum could be converted into an algorithm that they knew and could remember how to use. However, when, like Leah, algorithm clingers forgot how to use these skills (the rules of how to 'do' the sums), problems occurred. The skill of operating these algorithms is often learnt by rote, and children may have no underlying understanding of the meaning of the sums. When they forget the rules, they have no 'feel for number' that would enable them to rebuild the relevant algorithm or to solve the calculation in a different way. An earlier research study on able children's mental calculation strategies (see Murray 1999: 164) showed how a numerate child who forgot a fact (or a rule for an algorithm) was able to go on to calculate the answer using an effective strategy because he had a good underlying understanding of the number concepts involved. This knowledge operated then to give him a type of mathematical safety net. In contrast to this able child, if their rules failed to work then algorithm clingers seemed to have no back-up strategies beyond one-by-one counting.

Discussion

This was a small-scale project and consequently it is not possible to make generalisations from it to all low attainers. A further limitation of the study is that most of the assessment information used here is based on one-off assessments, focused only on decontextualised number calculations. It goes without saying that more extensive assessment would need to be undertaken in order to create full pictures of each child's mathematical knowledge and understanding in number, as well as in other key areas of mathematics. However, despite these acknowledged limitations to this study, it should be noted that some of the patterns found here in low attaining children's numeracy have also been identified in other studies over time (see, for example, Bird 2007; Denvir 1984; Hansen 2005; Haylock 1991, 2000; Houssart 2004).

Well on into Key Stage 2 the 9- and 10-year-olds in these case studies were still struggling with some basic mathematical calculations. They now trail long histories of being labelled as 'low achievers' and of working in the lowest group or set for mathematics, often under the guidance of a teaching assistant and alongside peers who also struggle with the subject. Assessed at level 2 in terms of the national curriculum levels (the 'average' level expected of a 7-year-old at the end of Year 2 is a 2A), not yet fully confident with addition and subtraction calculation strategies, with limited 'feel' for the size of numbers between 0 and 100, they have very low confidence levels and strong senses of already being defeated by the subject and of opting out.

However, despite all these factors they are nevertheless now being asked to work on a differentiated version of the standard Year 5 curriculum in which they encounter decimal and common fractions, negative numbers and number concepts such as multiplication and division. Some hard questions need to be asked about how much of this new knowledge such children are likely to understand. Learning objectives for low attainers may well be differentiated around the key content of the Year 5 curriculum, but we need to pose more fundamental questions about the pace of the mathematics curriculum, the normalised sequence of progression implied in it and its suitability for low attaining children. We have known for many years that the ways in which children learn mathematics are not always predictable or strictly hierarchical (see the seminal work of Brenda Denvir in 1984), but, in the case of these children, working on further into the complexities of mathematical knowledge and understanding whilst so much of early school mathematics remains insecure seems to be akin to trying to build a house on very shaky foundations.

It would be easy to attribute these children's situation to a long history of poor mathematics teaching. However, the reasons for such patterns of low achievement are undoubtedly complex and multi-factorial. None of the case study children received special needs support for their mathematics (or for any other subject), but this is not to say that they did not have undiagnosed learning needs in the subject. Provision for children's special mathematical learning needs is often less extensive than for literacy, and the issue of dyscalculia remains controversial and often unacknowledged in schools (Bird 2007), in ways that parallel the lack of recognition accorded to dyslexia in past decades. There is no suggestion in our data that any of the case study children in this study have recognised special educational needs in mathematics, including a learning disorder as severe as dyscalculia, but it is worth noting that quiet, unobtrusive children like Jodie-Anne and Leah will often slip under the teacher's 'radar', not least because they have a well-developed range of strategies for avoiding mathematics work. Jodie-Anne, for example, is adept at spending long periods of mathematics lessons sharpening pencils and looking for lost books.

These children, so far behind the rest of their year group in their mathematical learning, are not likely to be picked up by many of the kinds of 'catch up' programmes previously described in this chapter and designed to raise children 'up' one level before national tests. Yet they clearly need considerable help and attention if they are not to take their current mathematical heritage on into secondary schooling and then their adult lives. In order to achieve long-term patterns of success in the subject, it is crucial that these children's *confidence* and *competence* in numeracy are both raised. In other words, low attaining children need both *competence* in mathematics (as before, this term is used as a shorthand term for the knowledge and understanding of the relevant facts, skills, concepts and strategies) and the *confidence* in their own ability to use and apply this competence successfully, particularly generating an 'If I try I can do it' attitude to mathematics work.

As we have indicated, all the case study children had a history of finding mathematics difficult, dating back to the early years of their schooling. For many years there has been an understandable reluctance to 'label' children as struggling with mathematics in these early years. However, some initiatives in mathematics education (see, for example, Edge Hill University 2009; Wright *et al.* 2000) indicate that this well-meaning stance may lead to accumulating difficulties for the children concerned. In this study a number of the children, like Jodie-Anne, had 'trailed' difficulties with early mathematics, including learning to count, from the Reception class into Key Stage 1. As indicated earlier in this chapter, learning to count is a complex process for young children. It is also one of the foundation stones of mathematical learning. If children do not learn to count accurately and to use and apply this knowledge with confidence at an early stage in their schooling then their later mathematical development will inevitably be delayed.

Other children in the study, like Leah, had struggled with early mathematical language, both oral and written. Acquiring, understanding and applying mathematical language is an integral part of unlocking mathematics. Many children, not just those with English as an Additional Language needs, require additional help in understanding the complexities of this language and then being able to use it to explore their developing mathematical understanding.

Many low attaining children in Key Stage 2 show limited knowledge and understanding of two-digit place value. The variable rates at which children acquire knowledge of place value are well documented in studies reaching back to the Cockcroft Report (Cockcroft 1982). This body of research shows that some children 'trail' difficulties in developing secure conceptual knowledge of place value from Key Stage 1 well into Key Stage 2 and on into their secondary schooling. Yet this knowledge is fundamental to developing the 'feel for number' that enables children to estimate, to calculate by a variety of methods and to make judgements about whether or not their answers are correct. Without this basic understanding of how our number system works, low attainers have very limited opportunities to unlock the world of numeracy.

All curriculum guidance in mathematics places considerable emphasis on the importance of teaching and learning in these three key areas of learning to count, place value and developing age range-appropriate knowledge of mathematical language. However, the findings of this study point to the need for additional diagnostic assessment, and, when necessary, additional well-focused, teaching programmes for low attainers, in these three key areas. Such appropriate and well-focused interventions may help them to understand counting in all its diversity, to use, apply and understand a diversity of mathematical language and to develop conceptual understanding of place value. Early intervention may well prevent more complex patterns of underachievement persisting into later schooling. It is important that any interventions give well-targeted practice in these areas, but ideally in ways that do not repeat or reinforce the experiences which these children have had of years of previous mathematical failure.

This is very definitely not an avocation of a 'back-to-basics' approach. As we have argued earlier in this chapter, for us, the key to unlocking mathematics for low attainers is to focus on enhancing potential by developing both competence and confidence in personal attainment. A brief example of this approach to developing knowledge of place value is as follows: lower attaining children may often be asked to calculate with two- or perhaps three-digit numbers, when their peers are working with larger numbers, so emphasising their low attainment and potentially demotivating them further. Using digit cards to make 'big' numbers gives such children a sense of achievement, interest and engagement if they can make numbers in the hundreds of thousands and millions. Such activity needs to be carefully supported, so teachers might start by asking the children to make 27 with the cards, then to make that read 327, 5327, 45,327, 945,327 and finally 6,945,327, each time trying to read out loud the number they are making. With each successive 'turn', the children simply add the extra card, so this activity is not necessarily reliant on an understanding of place value. Teachers could then ask the children to swap the millions digit card with another and to say whether they have made the number bigger or smaller and by roughly how many million. Using calculators to practise place value is also effective. Children might be asked, for example, to key in a number such as 45 and change it to 35 without cancelling and entering 35.

Teaching approaches that explicitly connect different mathematical ideas and the ways in which they are represented are widely advocated in current guidance on teaching mathematics. Such guidance also advocates using a variety of appropriate resources to support the development of numeracy, emphasising that multi-sensory teaching approaches are important to enable all children to learn mathematics, but may well be of particular importance for low attainers.

The low attainment of the children in this study may have derived in part from their mono-dimensional understanding of how to tackle addition and subtraction problems. In this study, for Jodie-Anne counting on one-by-one remains her only method of addition; for Leah standard written algorithms that she struggled to recall served the same function; Damien, despite some alternative starting points for mental calculations, either recycled the same basic method of calculation or resorted to guess work. The potentially stimulating, rich and interconnected world of numeracy has become restricted, fragmented and probably deeply puzzling for them. Multi-sensory teaching approaches to mathematics enable connections within and across the world of numeracy to be made in meaningful ways.

A number of children who are judged to be low attaining in their numeracy work have strengths in other areas of mathematics work, for example in space and shape, using and applying mathematics and problem solving. The work of Bryant and Nunes (1996) emphasises that many children may have highly contextualised numeracy skills which they use in their lives outside school, but are often unable or unwilling to use these in the classroom. It is important then to provide low attaining children with a variety of contexts in which their developing mathematical knowledge can be meaningfully used and applied. Generating a sense of engagement in mathematical learning, with the aim of re-igniting interest in mathematics, is key. Placing calculations into a real-life context can give an enhanced sense of purpose for learning. And using calculators judiciously can offer low attaining children access to problem solving that they might not be able to tackle without such support. The ideas in Chapter 2, amended where necessary, offer some useful starting points for such mathematics.

The Williams Review (Williams 2008) emphasises the importance of classroom discussion of mathematics. Successive versions of national guidance for mathematics teaching have also identified the importance of children being able to articulate and discuss their mental mathematics strategies. The low attaining children in this study would almost certainly have had opportunities to attempt such discussions and to explore mathematical language, but these experiences may have been limited if they worked only with other children who also struggle with mathematics and its language. One idea for increasing children's confidence and competence in using and applying mathematical language is to set up paired experiences in which a low attaining child works with a more able peer, confident in explaining and discussing mental methods. These sessions have two aims: first, they aim to provide the low attainer with unpressurised opportunities to listen to a range of methods, hearing another child 'modelling' the use of this kind of mathematical language; second, they aim to give the low attainer regular practice in talking mathematically, perhaps hesitantly at first, but gradually becoming used to explaining their strategies, gaining confidence and enhancing mathematical vocabulary. At regular intervals the teacher or teaching assistant might also join in with these sessions to provide visual images of the strategies being described. For example, she or he could draw representations of the partitioning of two-digit numbers and of calculations using an empty number line.

A final point, the current national guidance on mathematics being implemented in a large number of English primary schools identifies the need for teachers and children to work to key learning objectives. Target setting for groups and individuals is part of this process. The principle of revisiting aspects of the numeracy curriculum at regular intervals is also implied by the commercial schemes of work used by many schools. These structures are basically sound, but, as we have argued above, the pace of the curriculum and the normalised sequence of progression implied in it may well need further adaptation for low attaining children.

It is important that low attaining children are set achievable and realistic targets that are clearly related to the outcomes of diagnostic assessments and to follow-up teaching programmes. As outlined above, there are key areas of early numeracy that need to be addressed in such programmes. However, as we also stress above, this is definitely not an advocation of a back-to-basics approach to assessment. It is important that the strengths that children have in using and applying knowledge in all areas of mathematics are assessed, recognised and used in target setting, as they offer important starting points for developing children's confidence in their mathematics work.

Low attaining children derive considerable benefits if their parents or carers are involved in and well informed about their mathematical learning. Some parents/carers may lack confidence in mathematics themselves; others may be uncertain of how they should be supporting their children or, like Leah's well-meaning parents, be badly advised. Such factors in parental/carer understanding of school mathematics may cause gaps, or even contradictions, to occur between the mathematics children are learning at school and that learnt at home or through out-of-school classes and home tutoring. Many schools endeavour to develop close relationships with parents/carers, ensuring that they understand how mathematics is now taught in schools and how they can help their children. In particular, involving parents/carers in setting and achieving the learning targets for low attainers is an important part of this process of partnership.

Conclusion

This chapter has drawn on the findings of a small-scale project to identify issues in low attaining children's mental calculations. It has used a definition of low attainers based partly on norm referenced judgements, but it has also asserted that, more importantly, the majority of these children are underattaining in relation to their own potential in mathematics. The current national focus is on raising the levels of attainment of these children in relation to their 'average' peers. Important as this issue may be on the educational agenda, we should not lose sight of the importance of simultaneously developing children's *individual* potential. We have argued that the key to unlocking mathematics for low attainers is to focus on enhancing potential by developing competence and confidence in personal attainment. In this way the foundations for long-term, ongoing, individual patterns of attainment can be built.

References

Bird, R. (2007) *The Dyscalculia Toolkit: Supporting Learning Difficulties in Mathematics*. London: Paul Chapman.

Bryant, P. and Nunes, T. (1996) *Children Doing Mathematics*. London: Wiley-Blackwell.

Cockcroft, W. H. (1982) *Mathematics Counts: Report of the Committee of Inquiry into the Teaching of Mathematics*. London: HMSO.

Denvir, B. (1984) 'The development of number concepts in low attainers in mathematics aged seven to nine years'. Unpublished PhD thesis, King's College, London.

Edge Hill University (2009) 'Every Child Counts: an introduction to Numbers Count'. Available at http://www.edgehill.ac.uk/everychildcounts/general/NumbersCount.htm.

Hansen, A. (ed.) (2005) *Children's Errors in Mathematics: Understanding Common Misconceptions in Primary Schools*. London: Learning Matters.

Haylock, D. (1991) *Teaching Mathematics to Low Attainers 8–12*. London: Paul Chapman.

Haylock, D. (2000) *Mathematics Explained for Primary Teachers*. London: Paul Chapman.

Houssart, J. (2004) *Low Attainers in Primary Mathematics: The 'Whisperers and the I Don't Knows'*. London: Routledge Falmer.

Murray, J. (1999) 'Mental mathematics', in Koshy, V., Ernest, P. and Casey, R. (eds) *Mathematics for Primary Teachers*, London: Routledge.

Williams, P. (2008) *Independent Review of Mathematics Teaching in Early Years Settings and Primary Schools*. London: HMSO.

Wright, R., Martland, J. and Stafford, A. (2000) *Early Numeracy: Assessment for Teaching and Intervention*. London: Paul Chapman.

Websites used in the compilation of this chapter and for further consultation

Department for Children Schools and Families, 'Independent Review of Mathematics Teaching in Early Years Settings and Primary Schools, Final Report, Sir Peter Williams, June 2008': http://publications.teachernet.gov.uk/eOrderingDownload/Williams%20Mathematics.pdf.

Department for Education, The National Strategies, 'NNS intervention programmes, Springboard materials', no date: http://nationalstrategies.standards.dcsf.gov.uk/primary/features/mathematics/intervention/springboard.

Department for Education, The National Strategies, 'Mathematics intervention materials: Wave 3', no date: http://nationalstrategies.standards.dcsf.gov.uk/node/20314.

Department for Education, The National Strategies, 'Supporting children with gaps in their mathematical understanding', April 2005: http://nationalstrategies.standards.dcsf.gov.uk/node/85218.

Department for Education, The National Strategies, 'Overcoming barriers in mathematics – helping children move from level 3 to level 4', November 2007: http://nationalstrategies.standards.dcsf.gov.uk/node/84818.

Department for Education, The National Strategies, 'Overcoming barriers in mathematics – helping children move from level 2 to level 3', March 2008: http://nationalstrategies.standards.dcsf.gov.uk/node/85232.

Department for Education, The National Strategies, 'Overcoming barriers in mathematics – helping children move from level 1 to level 2', January 2009: http://nationalstrategies.standards.dcsf.gov.uk/node/165293.

Department for Education, The National Strategies, 'Mathematics', no date: http://nationalstrategies.standards.dcsf.gov.uk/primary/primaryframework/mathematics/.

Edge Hill University, Every Child Counts, 'An introduction to Numbers Count', September 2008: http://www.edgehill.ac.uk/everychildcounts/general/NumbersCount.htm.

NFER, 'Trends in international mathematics and science study', 2007: http://www.nfer.ac.uk/research/projects/trends-in-international-mathematics-and-science-study-timss/.

US Department of Education, Institute of Education Sciences, National Centre for Education Statistics, 'Trends in international mathematics and science study', 2007: http://nces.ed.gov/timss/results07.asp.

Teaching mathematically promising children

Ron Casey

Caged birds do sing, but what would be their song if they are sometimes allowed to fly?

(Casey 1999: 14)

Introduction

In the past few decades there has been growing concern about the quality of provision for mathematically promising children in the UK. Straker, who led the National Numeracy Strategy in England in 1999, had stated in 1982 that:

> Gifted pupils have a great deal to contribute to the future well-being of the society, provided their talents are developed to the full during their formal education. There is a pressing need to develop the country's resources to the fullest extent, and one of our most precious resources is the ability and creativity of all children.
>
> (Straker 1982: 7)

The need for developing the mathematical promise of children was also asserted in *Mathematics Counts* (Cockcroft 1982), one of the most influential surveys in mathematics education within the UK:

> The statement that able children can take care of themselves is misleading; it may be true that such children can take care of themselves better than the less able, but this does not mean that they should be entirely responsible for their own programming; they need guidance, encouragement and the right kind of opportunities and challenges to fulfill their promise.
>
> (Cockcroft 1982: Paragraph 332)

The Cockcroft Report had highlighted that it was not sufficient for such children to be left to work through a textbook or a set of work cards; nor should they be given repetitive practice of processes that have already been mastered.

The challenge of making effective provision for children who have special abilities in mathematics is not specific to the UK. Even in the United States, where 'gifted' education has received a high profile over a long period, a committee was appointed by the National Council of Teachers of Mathematics in 1995 to consider ways of teaching mathematically promising pupils who are described as having the 'potential to become the leaders and problem solvers of the future' fifteen years after the following statement (NCTM 1980: 18) was made:

> The student most neglected, in terms of realizing full potential, is the gifted student in mathematics. Outstanding mathematical ability is a precious societal resource, sorely needed to maintain leadership in a technological world.

Recent developments in 'gifted and talented' education in England

Nearly three decades after the Cockcroft Report (1982) there are encouraging signs of developments that started with the launch of the 'Gifted and Talented' initiative by the government (DfEE 1997), sending a strong message that all schools should seek to create an atmosphere in which to excel is not only acceptable, but desirable. As part of the government initiative 'Excellence in Cities' (DfEE 1999), schools within a significant number of inner-city local education authorities were required to identify 5–10 per cent of their pupils as 'gifted and talented' and provide a distinct teaching and learning programme for them. More recently, the initiative has been extended to all schools and applies to the whole 4–18 age range. The need for subject-specific provision was also highlighted. Within mathematics, support documents have been provided from both the government Gifted and Talented strategy team and the Qualifications and Curriculum Authority on how to support the identification and teaching of mathematically gifted pupils. The Department for Education and Skills (2007) issued guidelines – referred to as the *National Quality Standards* – for identifying gifted and talented children and making appropriate provision for them. Schools in England are, at present, expected to demonstrate – with evidence – how these have been achieved.

In spite of the support documents provided for practitioners for meeting the needs of mathematically promising students, progress with practical implementation of the policy has been slow. The recently published, highly influential review into mathematics education by Sir Peter Williams (2008) highlighted that gifted and talented children were not stretched enough. Also, interestingly it has been pointed out by the National Centre for Excellence in Teaching Mathematics (NCETM 2009) in England that there has been a shortage of research into ways of making adequate provision for mathematically gifted students.

The contents of this chapter are informed by my experience of leading professional development projects supporting teachers to make provision for mathematically gifted students and designing resources for practical use, as part of the work of Brunel University's centre for the education of higher ability students. Three broad sections are provided:

1   understanding mathematical giftedness;

2   identification of mathematical giftedness;

3   aspects of effective provision.

Understanding mathematical giftedness

First, it is emphasised that terms such as 'mathematically gifted', 'mathematically promising', 'talented' and 'able' are used interchangeably and that there is no universally accepted definition or terminology in describing a special aptitude in children for mathematics. Koshy, Ernest and Casey (2009) explain that an ability is the quality of being able to do something; a natural or acquired skill or talent. Thus mathematical ability is the quality of being able to do mathematics, that is, being able to perform mathematical tasks and to utilise mathematical knowledge effectively. This could be in selected areas of mathematics or more widely. For school students, mathematical ability is normally manifested in accomplishing tasks related to the mathematics curriculum. The authors go on to say, however, that there is also a further dimension to mathematical ability, namely a potential or future-oriented skill: the capacity to learn and master new mathematical ideas and skills, as well as to solve novel and non-routine problems.

Theoretically, mathematical giftedness may be explained in terms of Howard Gardner's (1983, 1993) theory of multiple intelligences. Gardner proposes the existence of nine types of intelligences (based on neuropsychological analysis of human abilities). These are different and independent skills/abilities ('multiple intelligences') and include logical–mathematical, linguistic, visual–spatial, bodily–kinaesthetic, musical, interpersonal, intrapersonal, naturalistic and existential intelligences. Gardner's specific intelligence 'logical–mathematical intelligence' refers to a specific aptitude for mathematics. A useful way to conceptualise mathematical giftedness is to view giftedness in domain-specific terms with its own methodologies and procedures, as proposed by Van Tassel-Baska (1992).

As Koshy *et al.* (2009) state, at the forefront of any discussion of mathematical ability is the argument about whether or not it is innate, whether it is due to nature or nurture. Although still controversial, their view is that both are important. Krutetskii (1976), the Russian psychologist who conducted extensive research into mathematical giftedness, maintains that mathematical abilities are not innate, but are properties acquired in life. Krutetskii also wrote that some persons have inborn characteristics in the structure and functional features of their brains that are extremely favourable to the development of mathematical abilities. This suggests that, although actual mathematical abilities are not innate, some children will become more able than others because of inborn characteristics which are later developed and actualised into mathematical ability through subsequent development and experiences.

In terms of provision for mathematically gifted children, our work with gifted children at Brunel University draws on two principles. One is based on Vygotsky's central idea of the zone of proximal development (ZPD). Vygotsky (1978) defines ZPD as the distance between the actual developmental level, as determined by independent problem solving, and the level of potential development, as determined through problem solving under adult guidance or in collaboration with more capable peers. Koshy *et al.* (2009) explain that the ZPD lies beyond the area of problems that a child can do unaided, and includes the tasks that the child can do only with the help of a teacher, peer or parent. Through experience and development the child masters some of the abilities and tasks involved in the ZPD and they become part of the zone of accomplishment. At the same time some of the tasks that were unattainable, even with the help of others, now become accessible in the ZPD. Thus teaching plays a key role in bringing tasks and capabilities within reach. Second, in addressing the cognitive demand of learning tasks we have incorporated higher levels of thinking – analysis, synthesis and evaluation – proposed by Bloom's taxonomy (Bloom 1956), also taking note of Resnick's (1987) recommendations that higher order thinking involves providing children opportunities for multiple solutions and freedom of enquiry without predetermined outcomes.

Identification of mathematical giftedness

Attributes of the mathematically gifted and talented

Krutetskii (1976) developed a checklist of the key elements of mathematical thinking observed in the mathematically gifted. Koshy *et al.* (2009) lists the attributes as:

- An ability to formalise mathematical material, to isolate form from content, to abstract oneself from concrete numerical relationships and spatial forms, and to operate with formal structure – with structures of relationships and connections.

- An ability to generalise mathematical material, to detect what is of chief importance, abstracting oneself from the irrelevant, and to see what is common in what is externally different.

- An ability to operate with numerals and other symbols.

- An ability for 'sequential, properly segmented logical reasoning', which is related to the need for proof, substantiation and deductions.

- An ability to shorten the reasoning process, to think in curtailed structures.

- An ability to reverse a mental process (to transfer from a direct to a reverse train of thought).

- Flexibility of thought – an ability to switch from one mental operation to another; freedom from the binding influence of the commonplace and the hackneyed. This characteristic of thinking is important for the creative work of a mathematician.

- A mathematical memory. It can be assumed that its characteristics also arise from the specific features of the mathematical sciences, that this is a memory for generalisations, formalised structures and logical schemes.

- An ability for spatial concepts, which is directly related to the presence of a branch of mathematics such as geometry (especially the geometry of space).

The list of attributes shown in Table 7.1 draws on Krutetski's work and our own research in UK schools. It is useful for raising awareness of what to look for. For a teacher it would be useful to consider the children in a class with these attributes in mind and try to build up profiles of the children's mathematical abilities.

TABLE 7.1 Attributes of a mathematically gifted pupil

1.	Learns new ideas quickly
2.	Finds the work set for the class easy
3.	Understands challenging and abstract concepts with ease (e.g. decimals, negative numbers)
4.	Shows curiosity and asks many questions (usually reflective in nature)
5.	Is able to estimate accurately
6.	Is able to spot patterns and make connections between mathematical concepts
7.	Shows ability to analyse, reason and make some generalisations
8.	Is a fast information processor
9.	Enjoys learning mathematics
10.	Shows stamina and persistence
11.	Has the ability to be engaged in carrying out extended investigations
12.	Is able to transfer previous knowledge to new situations
13.	Produces unique and elegant solutions
14.	Enjoys solving problems and puzzles
15.	Recognises similar structures and solutions from what was previously learnt

An inclusive policy for the identification of mathematical talent

The need for flexibility in the identification process should be emphasised here. It is important to remember that identification of mathematical talent is not a simple process because children do not always show their true potential for all sorts of reasons. For example, lack of confidence, lack of parental support, difficult home circumstances, language problems or a lack of knowledge of basic skills to carry out mathematical work competently can all mask true mathematical promise in a child. Research does provide us with some pointers as to what to look and aim for. According to Sheffield (1999) the view of a fixed percentage of children demonstrating mathematical promise is outdated. As Sheffield points out, today we realise that high ability in mathematics is not something that students are born with and which will develop on its own. Mathematical promise needs to be developed and teachers must play a major role in the development of that promise. Sheffield reminds us that in the realisation of that potential, we need to consider four factors that will determine both the display and the fulfilment of high ability in mathematics. They are:

1 ability;
2 motivation;
3 belief;
4 experience.

Bearing in mind the complexity of the identification of mathematical talent, it is useful to use multiple sources for identification – both qualitative and quantitative information. For example, information can be gathered from the following sources:

- Tests – formative assessment and end-of-term and end-of-year results can be good indicators of high performance. However, it is worth remembering that some children who have high potential may not perform well in tests for various reasons.

- Information from parents, support teachers and peer groups. The last is useful in the case of children who may mask their true ability for fear of being given more work by the teacher.

- Qualitative information gathered through observations during lessons through both verbal and written responses to work. The quality of children's recordings often provides useful evidence of mathematical giftedness.

Finally, it is worth remembering that we can support children to develop their mathematical promise. Sheffield (1999) provides support for this view by citing recent brain functioning research that documents changes in the brain due to experiences. She cites Clarke's (1997: 8) assertion to support the argument:

No child is born gifted – only with the potential for giftedness. Although all children have amazing potential, only those who are fortunate enough to have opportunities to develop their uniqueness in an environment that responds to their particular patterns and needs will be able to actualize their abilities to high levels.

She reminds us that the brain grows and develops as it responds to challenging problems and mathematics is a perfect venue for this development.

The role of affect

In any attempt to identify mathematical giftedness attention should also be given to the role of affect. This is the central role of the affective domain, including motivation and attitudes. One simple model of this interaction is the 'success cycle' proposed by Ernest (1985) and illustrated in Figure 7.1.

As Ernest explains the success cycle has three components:

1   positive affect including attitudes and motivation towards mathematics;

2   effort, persistence and engagement with cognitively demanding tasks;

3   achievement and success at mathematical tasks.

The success cycle has no real beginning because these three components are linked cyclically, and each impacts positively on its successor. Taking (1) as a starting point we can say that students who have positive attitudes and beliefs about mathematics typically have high mathematical self-confidence and a good sense of mathematical self-efficacy. They enjoy doing mathematics and experience pleasure in the challenges

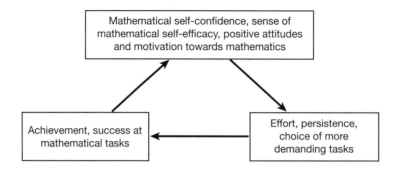

FIGURE 7.1 The success cycle.

it presents. This positive motivation leads to increased effort and persistence, more time on task and the choice of cognitively more demanding tasks in mathematics. Given appropriate opportunities the increased effort and work will give rise to continued success at mathematical tasks and overall achievement in mathematics. This sustains and further enhances positive attitudes, completing the success cycle and giving it more momentum. This gives rise to a virtuous, upward spiral.

Aspects of effective provision

We apply two basic principles when considering aspects of provision for mathematically promising students. The first is that education – which includes the learning of mathematics – should be an enriching experience for all children and that the starting point for talent development should be within the classroom. Second, it is accepted that giftedness is often domain specific and therefore provision should take the special abilities and aptitudes of the pupils into account. The content of the teaching programme within England and Wales is largely guided by the National Curriculum, which provides a framework for developing a knowledge base. It offers a structure and elements of progression. All children – including the very able – need a robust repertoire of facts and skills and fluency to be able to carry out enquiries efficiently. It cannot be assumed that all gifted children possess a robust framework of knowledge. Within the classroom, adaptations would be necessary. There will be pupils who may already know what is being taught to the rest of the class as well as some fast learners who are capable of mastering what is being taught to the rest of the class within a shorter time scale. These pupils would need to be provided with individual or group projects which require them to engage in tasks that offer higher cognitive demand. These tasks may highlight the need for learning advanced content and subject-specific methodology. At some stage individual guidance will need to be provided to equip them with these. Within the regular classroom, the option for individual students to pursue their special interests could also be provided. The time for undertaking these individual enquiries could be provided by some kind of *curriculum compacting* (Renzulli 1994), which involves streamlining material that has already been mastered by pupils.

It is also important to remember that identification and provision are parts of a two-way process, as shown in Figure 7.2; identification followed by provision is not always the best option. It is more likely that a teacher would identify a child with

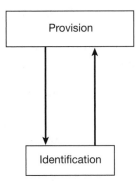

FIGURE 7.2 The provision–identification two-way process.

mathematical talent while working on a cognitively challenging task. However, it is also important that when children's mathematical promise is identified we make appropriate provision for them.

A framework for provision for higher ability mathematicians

In this section I will present a model that was devised for teachers (Casey 1999) who attended our professional development courses on teaching mathematically promising pupils at Brunel University. The model is built on firm foundations presented as theory and research earlier in this chapter. It should help to conceptualise the various aspects of mathematics teaching and at the same time provide a framework for assessing the quality of mathematical provision. This model, as shown in Figure 7.3, portrays the framework's features as a pentagon within a pentagon, with all the diagonals of the outer pentagon drawn. Each vertex of the inner pentagon has been given a label specifying a salient component of the learner's attributes or dispositions. Each vertex of the outer pentagon has a selected key concept assigned to it, highlighting the judgement that the named concept has a key role in the development of a deep

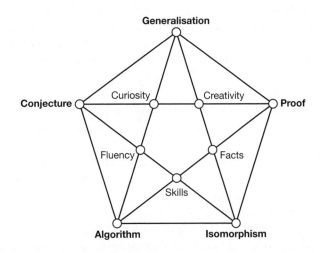

FIGURE 7.3 A key concepts model for teaching mathematics.

understanding of mathematics and in the design of learning tasks for able learners of mathematics.

The components of the model

First, let us consider the components of the model. Casey (1999) explains them as:

- the inner set of five components relating to the learner's dispositions – acquisition of *facts* and *skills*, *fluency*, *curiosity* and *creativity*;
- the outer set of five components relating to the methodology of the specific subject – mathematics in this case – *algorithm*, *conjecture*, *generalisation*, *isomorphism* and *proof*.

The first set of five components is selected to ensure a balance between the discipline and the practice needed by the children to acquire *facts* and *skills* and develop *fluency*. These are important components to master so that children can extend their knowledge and understanding further. It is possible that mathematically gifted children will learn facts, acquire skills and develop fluency faster than other children, but they do need these. At the same time children should be given freedom to pursue ideas that arouse their *curiosity* – in depth – which should help to develop a capacity for *creativity*. Without the inclusion of curiosity and creativity, the curriculum becomes a cage. Quite often we have seen children working through pages of textbooks and worksheets, repeating ideas they had mastered previously, which leads to a 'turning off' of the subject completely.

Now let us consider the outer five components of the model. Developing *algorithms* or procedures is essential for learning and doing mathematical tasks. Although there is a place for teaching children standard ways of performing mathematical calculations, they should be allowed freedom to develop and use their own algorithms. All too often we see children practising pages of calculations, which can often lead to boredom. In my experience a mathematically gifted child is capable of constructing personal algorithms that can be quite sophisticated and elegant.

An example of an investigation undertaken by 8-year-old Daniel, who attended one of our enrichment programmes that involved consecutive numbers, demonstrates the use of *conjectures*. After adding several sets of consecutive numbers, Daniel made the following conjectures:

- when you add two consecutive numbers the answer is always odd;
- when you add three consecutive numbers the answer is always odd.

After working on the second conjecture for a while and trying different numbers, Daniel revised his conjecture to 'when you add three consecutive numbers the answer is odd only if you start with an even number'.

In the above example a child should be encouraged to try several examples and then provide a *generalisation* which leads to a *proof* that 'the sum of two consecutive numbers is always odd'. Although an algebraic generalisation is not required at this stage, it can be provided algebraically as shown:

Let the first number be n.

Then the next number is $n + 1$.

The sum of the two consecutive numbers is $n + (n + 1) = 2n + 1$, which is always odd (as $2n$ is double, which must be even, so $2n + 1$, the number after $2n$, must be odd).

We have seen primary school children developing generalisations and developing proofs – often using words instead of letters.

The concept of *isomorphism* gives power to a young mathematician and some excitement. I have observed young children realising that seemingly different situations have the same underlying mathematical structure (detecting isomorphism) and feeling quite excited about it. Krutetski's (1976) research, which was referred to earlier, points to the fact that mathematically gifted children have a particular talent for detecting isomorphism. This is in fact an attribute that may be helpful in detecting high potential in mathematically able children.

The following two tasks should exemplify isomorphism:

A football tournament is to be arranged between five teams so that every team must play every other team once only. How many matches need to be arranged and played? Assume that the teams are Newcastle, Ipswich, Derby, Blackburn and Southampton.

A transport minister has decided that each of five towns needs to be directly linked to each of the other towns by newly built roads. How many new roads need to be built? Assume that the towns are Grimsby, Hastings, Newport, Plymouth and Stockport.

The facts and skills needed for this task include the ability to add consecutive numbers and the creativity to devise a recording system that reveals the isomorphism of the two situations.

The first situation is represented by Figure 7.4. An arc is drawn from one dot to another to represent a match arranged between the corresponding teams. To avoid double counting, as the matches are decided for a team, starting with Newcastle, the number of newly arranged matches is written near the dot representing the team. So, working clockwise, when it comes to Blackburn only one new match needs to be arranged. Hence the number of matches that needs to be organised is $4 + 3 + 2 + 1$, which is 10. Once again, the sum of the integers starting with 1 has arisen.

If the diagram for the football problem is changed so that Newcastle is replaced by Grimsby, Ipswich by Hastings, Derby by Newport, Blackburn by Plymouth and Southampton by Stockport, then the solution to the second problem follows from the diagram in exactly the same way as before. Figure 7.5 shows the representation of the road construction problem.

The two situations are isomorphic and the two diagrams, considered together, reveal and display the similarity of structure; a mathematically gifted child is very likely to identify the similarity of structure in these two situations and use or adapt any methods previously used to solve the problem.

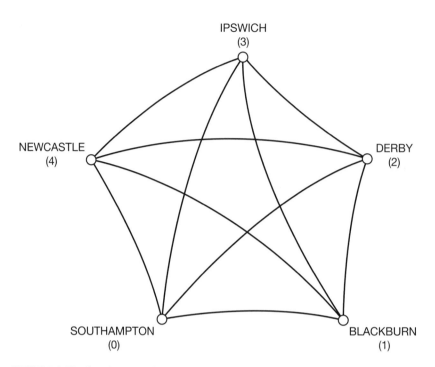

FIGURE 7.4 The first situation referring to the football problem.

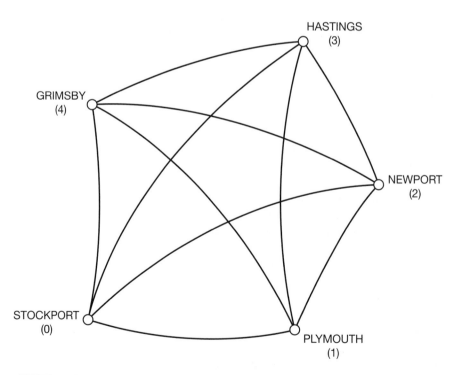

FIGURE 7.5 The second situation referring to the building of roads.

When considering whether a particular learning task is suitable for a class, group or individual child, the teacher could consider the following questions:

- What facts are needed to perform the task?

- What skills are required to engage in the task with at least some success?

- Will the facts and skills be remembered and used with sufficient fluency so as not to slow down the performance of the task?

- Will the task generate curiosity?

- Does the task have the potential to give opportunities for creativity?

- Does the activity provide opportunities for applying mathematical processes of conjecture, generalisation and proof?

- Will there be opportunities to develop and use their own algorithms and identify and make use of previously learnt ideas?

The curiosity and creativity aspects have been found to be the most difficult to judge in advance. With experience, both teachers and pupils can take pleasure in unexpected learning opportunities, as the three illustrations in Figure 7.6 will highlight.

Development of mathematical processes

Of course, there are other mathematical processes that we should encourage children to develop such as classifying, communicating, using symbols, estimating, reasoning, working systematically, justifying and checking. Attainment Target 1 in the Mathematics National Curriculum (DfEE/QCA 1999) lists the development of many of these processes as requirements.

The following example exemplifies how a primary school teacher, Jim Landers, implemented the key concepts model in his teaching of mathematics when his school joined Brunel University's 'Excellence in Mathematics Teaching' project. In a reflective article (Landers 1999: 7) Jim wrote:

> I realized that the most talented mathematicians are not always competent with basic facts and skills. I had to train my children to think, reason, conjecture, prove and generalize. Mathematics is a creative subject. Do I allow the children to be creative? Will a creative classroom be in conflict with the structured programme offered by the National Curriculum? It does not need to be.

Jim admitted that he had to develop a new style of working. There were times when he did not feel confident in his own mathematical knowledge, but he admitted that working with the children enhanced his own confidence and ability in guiding them.

Figure 7.6 shows how Emma, in Jim's class, carried out an investigation that involved working with polygons and diagonals. The whole class worked on the investigation, which started with a discussion of what polygons and diagonals are and how to draw diagonals. All of the children worked on this task and took the work to a level that they were able to. Emma and a few others used the processes of conjecture, working systematically, generalisation and proving the ideas. Curiosity and creativity are demonstrably

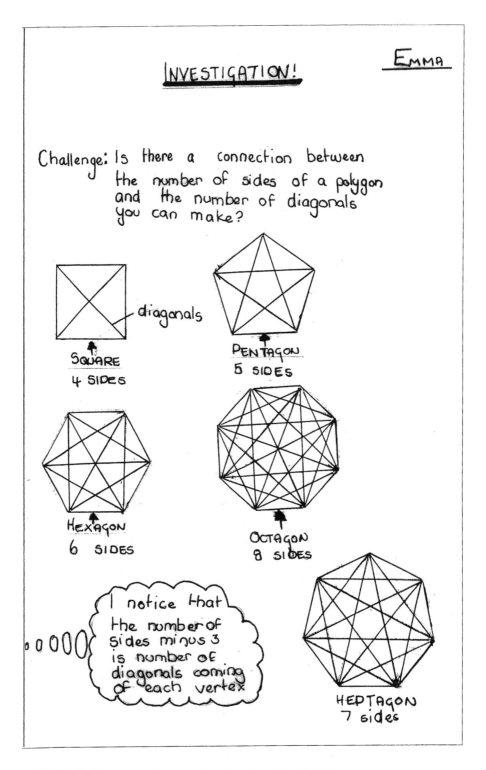

FIGURE 7.6 Three consecutive pages from Emma's mathematical diary.

Emma

Name Of Shape	Num Of Sides	Num Of Diagonals
Quadrilateral	4	2
Pentagon	5	5
Hexagon	6	9
Heptagon	7	14
Octagon	8	20

I noticed that the number of diagonals of a 4, 5, 6, 7, 8 sided shape increase in a pattern (2 + 3 = 5, + 4 = 9, + 5 = 14, + 6 = 20)

THE RULE

I think its sides − 3 × $\frac{sides}{2}$ = diagonal

eg: Pentagon 5 − 3 = 2 × 5 = 10 ÷ 2 = amount of diagonals: 5

This works with any shape

10 − 3 = 7 × 10 = 70 ÷ 2 = 35

9 − 3 = 6 × 9 = 54 ÷ 2 = 27

DECAGON
10 sides

NONAGON
9 sides

FIGURE 7.6 continued

137

I can make a formula from what
I know. This formula is:

FORMULA

$$(S - 3 \times \frac{S}{2} = d)$$

KEY
S = sides
d = diagonals

Now I can predict
any polygon's diagonals

CHART

Sides	Number of diagonals
20	170
21	189
22	209
23	230
40	740
80	3,080
160	12,560
320	50,720

What I notice about
My Chart
The first 4 numbers (20, 21, 22, 23) still
go up in a pattern. 170 + 19 = 189 + 20 = 209
+ 21 = 230. Strangely, in my pattern, double
the number (sides) is not double the diagonals

FIGURE 7.6 continued

present. One other aspect that children were trained to use was their metacognitive skills in reflecting and recording their findings, as can be seen in Figure 7.6.

Choice and design of tasks

As classroom provision involves providing suitable tasks for the children, it would be appropriate to consider the following list of features that were found useful in the design of activities by teachers who have worked with us. Along with the criteria given as part of the key concepts model, these provide a framework for selecting and evaluating activities.

Activities should:

- be set within motivating and interesting contexts – we found that tasks relating to real-life situations were particularly effective;
- help to draw on previous knowledge of content and structure and enable children to recognise similar structures in different investigations (isomorphism);
- provide opportunities for discussion and communication;
- have multi-level outcomes – this makes them suitable for use with a wider range of abilities providing opportunities for children to demonstrate their mathematical ability;
- help the development of mathematical processes such as making conjectures, reasoning, generalising and offering proof;
- include problems with multiple solutions and methodologies for solving;
- provide opportunities for the pursuit of curiosity and creativity;
- encourage reflection and metacognition;
- offer richness, depth and opportunities for learning;
- encourage personal research, leading to learning advanced content;
- provide opportunities for continuous assessment.

In this section I present four activities that we designed for primary school teachers to use as part of a professional development course (Koshy 2008, 2011). These were trialled by teachers and were found to be effective for use with able mathematicians. We designed two types of activities: *short challenges and puzzles*, which encourage mental strategies and can be used as starters, and extended *investigations*, which may take more than one lesson or could become part of homework.

I suggest you study and review these activities with the desirable features of activities for challenging gifted mathematicians in mind. Which of the features do these offer? Teachers used all of the following activities with children aged from 9 to 10. Children worked either in pairs or in small groups. In some cases (when the children were set according to their abilities, for example) the activities were given to the whole class; sometimes an easier version of the activities was given to the rest of the class while the more able worked on these activities.

Children solved the 'Challenging Problems' (Figure 7.7) using a range of problem-solving strategies: applying logic, trial and error, drawing diagrams, reasoning, making decisions, discussing and refining their previous ideas. The solutions – eighty of each coin, sixteen tulip bulbs and five jumpers at £13.00 each and four T-shirts at £10 each – were arrived at with some excitement. Each problem took about ten minutes to solve.

The 'Dream Bedroom' problem (Figure 7.8), which involved optimisation, estimation and many calculations, generated the most excitement and discussions and perhaps was one of the most motivating tasks. Teachers attributed this to its meaningful, real-life context and the opportunities for making decisions – especially if an online catalogue was used. Planning, meaningful problem solving, recording, scale drawing and discussions took place.

While working on the 'Mystic Rose' investigation (Figure 7.9) children recognised similarities with previous work they had carried out, which involved working systematically, drawing tables and looking for patterns and relationships between the number of points on the circle and the number of lines before arriving at a generalisation – initially in words and then shown by the teacher written as

$$n(n-1)/2.$$

What was required for the 'True, False or Rewrite' activity (Figure 7.10) was found to be the most challenging by the children, as the format of the activity required them to make decisions on the basis of trying several examples, reasoning and revising their initial decisions. Making changes to the statements and rewriting them was found to be quite challenging. Arriving at the solutions – true, false, true, true, true, true, true and false – took time and careful training. Recordings made by the children showed a sophisticated level of mathematical thinking and challenge.

Aspects of organisation

When discussing aspects of provision it is also important to consider the different kinds of organisational structures commonly used to address the needs of mathematically able children. The first is *setting* pupils according to their mathematical ability, usually into three sets of 'top', 'middle' and 'lower' abilities, which is commonly used in schools. The main advantage of setting is to reduce the complexity of planning and teaching children within a wide range of abilities. Teachers justify the choice of setting as a way of 'not holding up the bright child' while teacher time is made available for children who may be struggling. In a top set it may be easier to organise in-depth discussions and teach more advanced concepts. Research has shown (Kulik 1992) that grouping by ability helps higher ability learners. It is also easier to increase the pace of teaching for a higher ability group of children. However, there are drawbacks in using the setting strategy, as highlighted by teachers who have worked with us, which include that the rest of the children miss out on the expertise of the most able and there is a lack of both suitable training for teachers and resources to teach the top sets.

If pupils are identified as exceptionally able in mathematics the strategy of *acceleration* is sometimes considered. For the practitioner, making sense of the word 'acceleration' and what it entails is in itself a challenge. Although many interpretations exist, the most common one involves either moving children up to a class of higher age

Coin mystery

A total of £48 was made up of an equal number of 50p and 10p coins.

? How many of each coin were there?

Spring gardening

A gardener had five days in which he had to plant 200 tulip flower bulbs.

On each day after the first day, he planted 12 more bulbs than on the previous day, picking up speed due to his practice. He completed the task at the end of the fifth day.

? How many bulbs did he plant on the first day?

Natalie's T-shirt

Natalie bought jumpers for £13 each, and some T-shirts for £10 each.

She spent a total of £105.

? How many of each did she buy?

FIGURE 7.7 Starter activity: a set of problems.

You have a chance to plan a dream bedroom. Your teacher will give you a page from a catalogue that shows items of furniture and other luxuries. Floor covering and curtains will be in the room, but you must choose a bed and any other items you wish to buy.

It is a good idea to discuss your idea with a friend before you decide what to buy and where you will place everything.

Your total budget is £900; you can go over or under you budget by £50.

Make a list of the items you will buy and an approximate calculation of your total. You can buy as many cuddly toys and pictures as you like. No calculators are allowed at this stage. Your teacher will tell you when to use a calculator to find out how well you have done within your budget.

You must also draw a plan (to scale) of your room and where you will place all the items you will be buying. Doors and windows are marked.

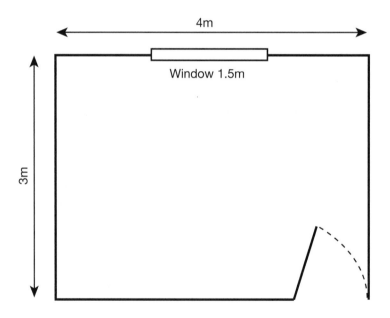

FIGURE 7.8 Investigation: furnish your dream bedroom.

Join the points on a circle to every other point.
If you join 12 points you will get an intricate pattern.

Investigate the relationship between the number of lines on the circle and the number of lines required to join all the points to each other.

? Can you find a general rule?

2 points = 1 line   3 points = 3 lines

4 points = 6 lines   5 points = 10 lines

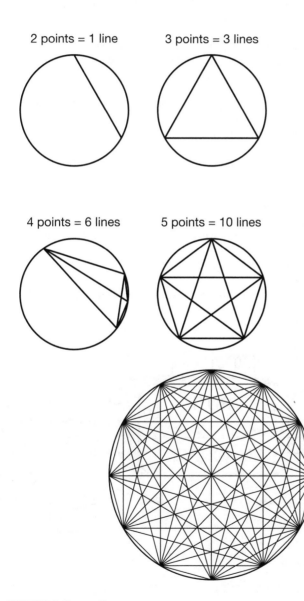

FIGURE 7.9 The mystic rose.

Decide which of the following statements are true. Show your reasons for your decisions. If they are false, make changes or polish the statement, as required, to make the statements true.

A. Given a starting number divide it by another number and multiply the result by the same number, so you finish with the number you started with.

B. Find the cube root of a number and then the square root of the result. Take the number you obtain, multiply it by itself five times and you get the number you started with.

C. Given three numbers, multiplying the first two and dividing the result by the third gives the same result as dividing the first by the third and multiplying the result by the second.

D. Start with a number. Multiply it by itself six times. Find the square root of the result and the cube root of what you get. The number you obtain is the number you started with.

E. Divide any number, in turn, by each of its prime factors. You will always finish with the number 1.

F. Start with a three-digit number. Express it as the product of its prime factors. Square each of their factors, multiply the results and then find the square root of the result. You will get the original three-digit number.

G. The cube of a number is larger than its square.

H. The total of six consecutive numbers will always be divisible by 6.

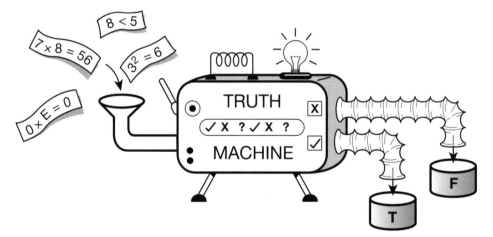

FIGURE 7.10 True, false or rewrite.

group or teaching them content designed for older children. Advocates of this strategy (Stanley 1991; Van Tassel-Baska 2001) encourage it as a teaching style which provides intervention that is intense and at a faster rate. A system developed by Johns Hopkins University in the United States provides accelerated learning programmes for pupils who are selected on the basis of mathematics and verbal reasoning. These pupils are provided with teaching programmes that are described as providing an *optimal match* for their ability, and currently they serve thousands of students internationally (Van Tassel-Baska 2001). In the UK, however, the acceleration strategy has been relatively unpopular (Fielker 1997; UK Mathematics Foundation 2000), perhaps as a result of press coverage of emotional and social difficulties and pressures experienced by pupils who have been radically accelerated by *grade skipping* or early entry to university. Enrichment for depth is recommended as a more popular option in which pupils are encouraged to participate in either individual or group projects.

Sheffield (1999) advises us that enrichment for added breadth is a way forward, which involves providing extension work that enriches the official curriculum by requiring deeper understanding of standard material (e.g. by insisting on a higher level of fluency in working with fractions, ratio, algebra or problem solving). Mathematics educationists, such as Fielker (1997), as mentioned previously, have expressed concern with the acceleration strategy by asserting that in this model pupils do not learn more about mathematics and what they do is merely learn the same mathematics sooner.

This, Fielker says, does not seem to fulfil the needs of the more able, who deserve something better. In this context it is interesting to note that Sheffield (1999), the chairperson of the US Task Force looking into provision for mathematically promising students, urges us to drop the *acceleration versus enrichment* debate and suggests that what we need to take into account is the depth of mathematics being learned. She reminds us of the criticism raised by Schmidt *et al.* (1996) that the US mathematics curriculum can be described as a mile wide and an inch deep; that is, US students often learn a little bit about everything (and repeat that little bit for years) without exploring the rich depths of mathematics. Sheffield's three-dimensional model (Figure 7.11), and her assertion that mathematically promising pupils should look not only at changing the rate or the number of mathematical offerings, but also at changing the depths or complexities of the mathematical investigations, was welcomed by the teachers who worked with us.

In the context of her involvement in other projects for gifted children, Koshy (2001) found that many of the mathematical tasks offered to very able mathematicians included both enrichment and acceleration in the sense that when pupils were motivated to carry out a complex and in-depth investigation they often sought new and more advanced knowledge.

The role of questioning

The quality of mathematical provision can be enhanced by the nature of the questioning techniques used. In an illuminating chapter on developing mathematical creativity Sheffield (2009: 87) stated that 'The ability to ask questions and provide opportunities that lead students to create and make sense of mathematics remain a major challenge

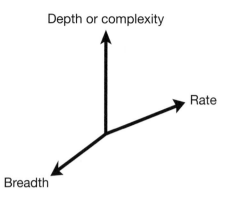

FIGURE 7.11 The three-dimensional model.

for teachers'. Sheffield contends that, in this complex world, it is not sufficient for teachers to teach students to memorise rules and formulae and answer mathematical questions as in the past and also that it is not enough for teachers to ask probing questions; students must also learn to ask questions that add depth and interest to mathematics. The type of questions that Sheffield recommends are:

- *Who?* Who can state that in your own words? Who used a different method or has a different solution? Who is right? Who agrees or disagrees?
- *What* or what if? What sense can I make of this problem? What patterns do I see in this data? What generalisations might I make from the patterns? What proof do I have? What if I change one or more parts of the problem?
- *When?* When does this work? When does it not work?
- *Where?* Where did this come from? Where might I find additional information?
- *Why?* Why does that work? If it does not work, why not?
- *How?* How does this relate to other problems or patterns that I have seen? How does it differ? How does it relate to real-life situations or models?

Sheffield gives an example of engaging children in in-depth discussions from the 'Mentoring Mathematical Minds' project she led for primary age children. The project team encouraged children to investigate one problem a day, probing deeply and posing their own questions related to the initial problem. They were expected to create their own methods of solution and to share and discuss these with classmates, learning from each other. One fascinating example is given. Children were asked: 'Which of the shapes does not belong?' (see Figure 7.12). The first student would name one of the shapes and then justify the selection using what they knew about the properties of polygons. The second student might then rephrase the response from the first student and state reasons for agreeing or disagreeing with this selection. Once this shape has been discussed, students were asked to select another shape and have similar discussions. Fluency, flexibility and originality were encouraged as students developed a deep understanding of the properties of polygons.

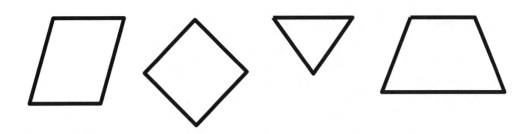

FIGURE 7.12 Which shape does not belong?

According to Watson and Mason (1998) questions such as 'How did you?', 'Why does?' and 'What if?' are typical questions intended to provoke children into becoming aware of mathematical thinking processes, into encountering convincing and proving and into exploration. These are processes we need to develop in all children, but mathematically able children are capable of engaging in these processes more skilfully.

Information technology

Information technology can provide a range of excellent opportunities for the promising young mathematician. Computers and calculators offer tools for carrying out independent mathematical explorations for all students, but they enable the gifted student to investigate ideas in considerable depth and solve complex and real problems. Computer programming and the use of programmable turtles can encourage the use of higher order thinking, exercise creativity and develop mathematical processes. The internet can provide information about resources, such as the very popular NRICH site (http://nrich.maths.org), and details of competitions and mathematics clubs. A group of young students who worked with us at the university used the internet to research into complex mathematical ideas and study the biographies of eminent mathematicians. Calculators enable children to solve problems that involve large numbers and complex real-life data. The following three recent examples of problems were carried out by 7- to 8-year-olds:

1   I am thinking of the number 140,556, which is the product of three consecutive numbers. What are the three numbers?
2   Your friend says you have been alive for one million seconds. Do you think it is true?
3   A £20 note weighs 1 g. How many kilograms would £2 million in £20 notes weigh?

With the help of a calculator, the children worked out these problems correctly. The calculator took away the drudgery of calculations so that the children could focus on the processes of problem solving and they produced impressive recordings.

Conclusion

The education of young gifted mathematicians in the UK is at a critical stage. As a result of recent policy initiatives and reviews on mathematics education there is now a real opportunity to develop systems that can benefit our promising mathematicians. Ultimately the effectiveness of any programme for gifted children will depend on the level of real support offered to teachers in their efforts in making effective provision. It is also important to remember that in the context of actualising mathematical talent we need to consider identification and provision not as separate elements but as a two-way interacting process. Smith's (2004) report to the government into the state of mathematics in England highlights the situation of a long decline in the numbers of young people continuing to study mathematics post-16. It draws attention to possible factors underlying this decline. Among those are the perceived poor quality of teaching and learning, the failure of the curriculum to excite interest and provide appropriate motivation and many young people's perception of mathematics as 'boring and irrelevant'. I hope the contents of this chapter will support practitioners in some small way towards offering young talented mathematicians opportunities to recognise the beauty of mathematics and see it as a creative discipline.

References

Bloom, B. (1956) *Taxonomy of Educational Objectives*. Harlow: Longman.

Casey, R. (1999) 'A key concepts model for teaching and learning mathematics', *Mathematics in School*, 28 (3): 29–31.

Clarke, B. (1997) 'No child is born gifted: creating and developing unlimited potential', *Parenting for High Potential*, March: 8–11.

Cockcroft, W. H. (1982) *Mathematics Counts: Report of the Committee of Inquiry into the Teaching of Mathematics in Schools*. London: Her Majesty's Stationery Office.

Department for Education and Skills (2007) *National Quality Standards for Gifted and Talented Education*. London: DfES.

DfEE (Department for Education and Employment) (1997) *Excellence in Schools*. London: DfEE.

DfEE (Department for Education and Employment) (1999) *Excellence in Cities*. London: DfEE.

DfEE/QCA (Department of Education and Employment/Qualifications and Curriculum Authority) (1999) *Mathematics: The National Curriculum for England*. London: DfEE.

Ernest, P. (1985) 'Special educational needs in mathematics', *CASTME Journal*, 6 (1): 22–28.

Fielker, D. (1997) *Extending Mathematical Ability through Whole-Class Teaching*. London: Hodder and Stoughton.

Gardner, H. (1983) *Frames of Mind*. New York: Basic Books.

Gardner, H. (1993) *Multiple Intelligences*. New York: Basic Books.

Koshy, V. (2001) *Teaching Mathematics to Able Children*. London: David Fulton.

Koshy, V. (2008) *Enrichment Activities for Mathematically Gifted Children, 9–11*. Twickenham: Elephas.

Koshy, V. (2011) *Enrichment Activities for Mathematically Gifted Children, 7–9*. Twickenham: Elephas.

Koshy, V., Ernest, P. and Casey, R. (2009) 'Mathematically gifted and talented learners: theory and practice', *International Journal of Mathematical Education in Science and Technology*, 40 (2): 213–218.

Krutetskii, V. A. (1976) *The Psychology of Mathematical Abilities in School Children*. Chicago: University of Chicago Press.

Kulik, J. A. (1992) *An Analysis of Research on Ability Groupings: Historical and Contemporary Perspectives*. Storrs, CT. The National Research Centre on the Gifted and Talented, The University of Connecticut.

Landers, J. (1999) 'The pursuit of excellence in my classroom', *Mathematics in School*, 28 (3): 7–9.

NCETM (National Centre for Excellence in Teaching Mathematics) (2009) http://www.ncetm.org.uk.

NCTM (National Council of Teachers of Mathematics) (1980) *An Agenda for Action: Recommendations for School Mathematics of the 1980s*. Reston, VA: NCTM.

Renzulli, J. (1994) *Schools for Talent Development: A Practical Plan for School Improvement*. Mansfield Center, CT: Creative Learning Press.

Resnick, L. B. (1987) *Education and Learning to Think*. Washington, DC: National Academy Press.

Schmidt, W., McKnight, C. and Raizen, S. (1996) *A Splintered Vision: An Investigation of US Mathematics and Science Education*. Washington, DC: US National Research Center.

Sheffield, L. (1999) 'Serving the needs of the mathematically promising', in Sheffield, L. (ed.) *Developing Mathematically Promising Students*. Reston, VA: NCTM.

Sheffield, L. (2009) 'Developing mathematical creativity – questions may be the answer', in Leikin, R., Berman, A. and Koichu, C. (eds) *Creativity in Mathematics and the Education of Gifted Students*. Rotterdam: Sense Publications.

Smith, A. (2004) *Making Mathematics Count: The Report of Professor Adrian Smith's Inquiry into Post-14 Mathematics Education*. London: Stationery Office.

Stanley, J. (1991) 'An academic model for educating the mathematically talented', *Gifted Child Quarterly*, 35: 36–42.

Straker, A. (1982) *Mathematically Gifted Pupils*. Harlow: Longman.

UK Mathematics Foundation (2000) *Acceleration or Enrichment: Serving the Needs of the Top 10% in School Mathematics*. Birmingham: School of Mathematics, Birmingham University

Van Tassel-Baska, J. (1992) *Planning Effective Curriculum for Gifted Learners*. Denver: Love Publishing.

Van Tassel-Baska, J. (2001) 'The talent development process: what we know and what we don't know', *Gifted Education International*, 16: 20–28.

Vygotsky, L. (1978) *Mind in Society*. Cambridge, MA: Harvard University Press.

Watson, A. and Mason, J. (1998) *Questions and Prompts for Mathematical Thinking*. Derby: Association of Teachers of Mathematics.

Williams, P. (2008) *Independent Review of Mathematics Teaching in Early Years Setting and Primary Schools*. London: DCSF.

Assessing mathematical learning

Valsa Koshy and Sarah Jackson-Stevens

Teachers have always assessed children's learning in a variety of ways. Classroom assessment may take place as informal or structured observations or as written tests. Whatever method of assessment is used, the main purpose of assessment remains the same – to provide information about children's learning. What has been changing is the practitioners' conception of assessment as something that teachers imposed *on* their children to a process in which they involved children. In the past, assessment has been seen by many – teachers, children and parents – as something that was carried out *after* teaching to check what has been learnt and make judgements; fear of failure and negative comparisons had been part of that image. During the past decade, increasing emphasis has been placed on the principle that assessment is strongly linked with learning and that it is a process that involves the active participation of both teachers and children.

What do we mean by assessment? What does it do? Assessment can be described as the process by which teachers gain an understanding of the nature and level of children's knowledge and understanding of what was taught, as well as a sense of the child's capability to learn. Assessment also provides insights into what progress is being made by the children. Supported by research (Black and Wiliam 1998) it has been established that assessment has a critical role in the process of learning and teaching, children's motivation and learning power. Good quality assessment should provide the teacher with useful insights into not only what to teach, but also what teaching styles to employ, the nature of the tasks they select and what organisational structure to use.

In the UK the shift in our thinking from considering assessment as a teacher-driven and one-sided activity that involves testing at the *end of learning* something to one that consists of ongoing gathering of information in a number of ways and using that information to plan future learning of the children has been greatly influenced by *Inside the Black Box*, the seminal work of Black and Wiliam (1998), which places more emphasis on the formative aspects of learning. This work and subsequent publications by the Assessment Reform Group (2002) started a new dawn in the history of assessment known as Assessment for Learning (AfL), which is the basis of and an integral part of policy recommendations for assessment practices. Assessment for learning is carried out with the purpose of informing planning before teaching and learning. In this model the teacher continually reviews the learning and does not just measure what has been learnt. Black, Harrison, Marshall and Wiliam (2003) define Assessment for Learning as any assessment for which the priority in its design is to serve the purpose of promoting pupils' learning. It differs from assessment designed primarily to serve the purposes of accountability, or of ranking or of certifying competence.

In this chapter we aim to explore the following aspects of assessment:

1   What are we assessing in mathematics?
2   What types of assessment should we use?
3   How do we enhance our assessment practices and translate the principles into classroom practice?

We will attempt to explore the above questions using examples either from our own experiences or from what we have seen and know to be judged as 'good practice' in assessment by authoritative sources.

The important role of the teacher in the process of assessment is crucial. In an influential recent report by Sir Peter Williams on the teaching of mathematics (Williams 2008) the author stresses the central role of effective teacher pedagogy with regard to assessment:

> As teachers' own knowledge of mathematics, enthusiasm for the subject and beliefs about teaching and learning impact on their classroom practice, it is important that teachers reflect on the impact of the assessment for learning model on their teaching. (p. 63)

The report goes on to say that

> First and foremost, pedagogy must be learner-centred, in the sense that it is responsive to the needs of the particular children being taught through effective diagnostic assessment and broader adoption of Assessment for Learning. (p. 63)

To set the context of what follows in this chapter we draw on the ten principles for assessment for learning provided by the Assessment Reform Group (2002). Assessment for learning should:

1   be part of effective planning for teaching and learning;
2   focus on how pupils learn;
3   be recognised as central to classroom practice;
4   be regarded as a key professional skill for teachers;
5   be sensitive and constructive because any assessment has an emotional impact;
6   take account of the importance of learner motivation;
7   promote commitment to learning goals and shared understanding of the criteria by which pupils will be assessed;
8   provide constructive guidance for learners about how to improve;

9   develop learners' capacity for self-assessment and recognising their next steps and how to take them;

10 recognise the full range of achievement of all learners.

What are we assessing in mathematics?

A good starting point for consideration before we carry out assessment is to ask ourselves two all-important questions: What is mathematics? and What are our objectives in teaching mathematics?

Drawing on an illuminating discussion of these by Ernest (2000), which takes into account the objectives of teaching mathematics stated in the Cockcroft Report (1982) and Her Majesty's Inspectorate (1985), we will discuss the practical implications of assessing the different objectives. We need to assess whether children:

- know their mathematical facts and language;
- have acquired the necessary mathematical skills with understanding;
- appreciate the interconnectedness of mathematical ideas;
- have developed a robust conceptual understanding of mathematical ideas;
- can employ effective strategies for problem solving in mathematics;
- have a positive attitude towards the subject.

These are discussed in the following sections.

Assessing facts

What are mathematical facts? Children need to learn the correct names of numbers and shapes and mathematical terms such as multiplication and fraction. They need to recognise mathematical symbols such as $+$, $-$, % and so on. Recall of number bonds such as $8 + 6 = 14$ or $7 \times 5 = 35$ is important too. All of these are important as they are 'the basic atoms of knowledge which fit into a larger and more meaningful system of facts' (Ernest 2000: 4). For example, in the National Curriculum for England (DfEE/QCA 1999), children are expected to *read and write numbers and learn the use of symbols.* There are many opportunities during the mathematics lesson when the acquisition of facts can be assessed. For example, during the introduction or a plenary session, we can ask targeted questions that will highlight any gaps in children's recall and recognition of facts. It is possible to organise 'fact books' and ask children to record their number facts on a teaching topic regularly and take any action necessary. When we assess knowledge it is important to remember that a child who can recite multiplication tables correctly, read numbers accurately and write fractions correctly does not necessarily understand the principles behind the facts or how they have been arrived at. In order to assess we will need to gather more evidence through different kinds of questions that elicit explanations.

Assessing skills

The Cockcroft Report describes skills as an integral part of learning mathematics:

> Skills include not only the use of the number facts and the standard computational procedures of arithmetic and algebra, but also of any well established procedures which it is possible to carry out by the use of a routine. They need not only to be understood and embedded in the conceptual structure but also to be brought up the level of immediate recall or fluency of performance by regular practice. (Cockcroft 1982: Paragraph 240)

Performing calculations and measuring using a ruler or a protractor require the use of learnt skills. Observing children at work or listening to them verbalise their methods during a lesson or at a plenary session provides valuable insights into their ways of thinking. The steps they take or the mistakes they make can often show the teacher any patterns of misunderstandings and misconceptions. Observations can also show whether children are adopting the most sensible and efficient strategies to carry out calculations. An important point to remember here is that many of the children's mistakes originate from misunderstood rules. Alternatively they could be the result of children constructing their own set of rules without understanding the basic principles. Mistakes and misconceptions can often be corrected easily if action is taken promptly. Look at the examples in Figure 8.1 of some common mistakes that children make and ask yourself, if these mistakes are spotted while marking children's work, what information do they give you about a child's competence with the particular skills? It is useful to also consider what action should be taken.

A comprehensive discussion of children's mistakes and misconceptions in mathematics (Koshy 2000) should provide further illumination of how analysing mistakes can contribute to formative assessment of mathematical learning.

Assessing conceptual understanding

Conceptual structures are described in the Cockcroft Report (1982) as richly interconnecting bodies of knowledge. A robust conceptual understanding is necessary for children to become competent mathematicians. HMI (1985: 15) explains the importance of the interrelationships between concepts:

> No concept stands alone: for example, subtraction is linked with addition, multiplication is linked with addition and percentages are linked with fractions and in fact, each concept is linked with many other aspects of mathematics. Indeed, being good at mathematics is dependent of the ability to recognise relationships between one concept and another.

Research carried out at King's College (Askew *et al.* 1997) also suggests that effective teachers of numeracy emphasise the interconnections between concepts. As conceptual structures grow and strengthen as the child learns more mathematics, there is a

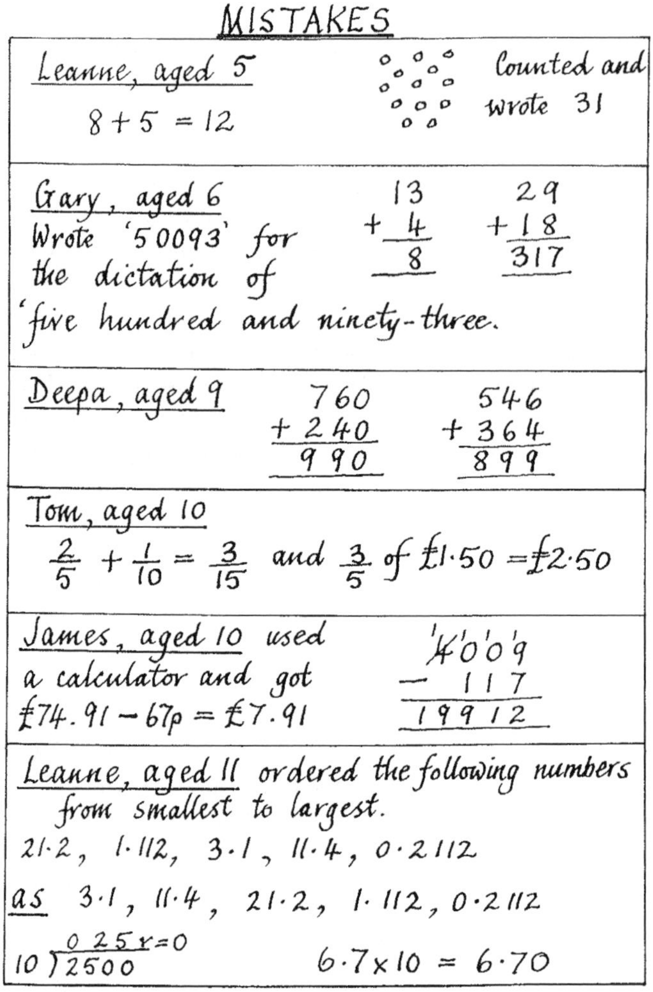

MISTAKES

Leanne, aged 5 $$8 + 5 = 12$$	°°°°° °°° °°° °°°	Counted and wrote 31
Gary, aged 6 Wrote '50093' for the dictation of 'five hundred and ninety-three.	$$\begin{array}{r} 13 \\ + 4 \\ \hline 8 \end{array}$$	$$\begin{array}{r} 29 \\ + 18 \\ \hline 317 \end{array}$$
Deepa, aged 9	$$\begin{array}{r} 760 \\ + 240 \\ \hline 990 \end{array}$$	$$\begin{array}{r} 546 \\ + 364 \\ \hline 899 \end{array}$$
Tom, aged 10 $$\frac{2}{5} + \frac{1}{10} = \frac{3}{15} \quad \text{and} \quad \frac{3}{5} \text{ of } £1.50 = £2.50$$		
James, aged 10 used a calculator and got $£74.91 - 67p = £7.91$	$$\begin{array}{r} \cancel{4}\,0\,0\,9 \\ - \quad 1\,1\,7 \\ \hline 1\,9\,9\,1\,2 \end{array}$$	
Leanne, aged 11 ordered the following numbers from smallest to largest. $21.2, \ 1.112, \ 3.1, \ 11.4, \ 0.2112$ as $3.1, \ 11.4, \ 21.2, \ 1.112, \ 0.2112$ $$10\,\overline{)2500}^{\,0\,25\,r=0} \qquad 6.7 \times 10 = 6.70$$		

FIGURE 8.1 Examples of mistakes.

need for assessing if there are any gaps in the understanding of concepts and whether action needs to be taken. When a child exhibits knowledge of facts or skills, it is not always easy to evaluate whether what has been learnt has been superficial or learnt by rote. Assessment of conceptual understanding may take longer than the assessment of facts and skills (although successful performance will depend on the acquisition of the former). For example, it is relatively easier to assess if a child recognises a number name, or the terms 'hundreds', 'tens' and 'units', than to assess if she or he understands the principle of place value. Similarly, it takes more careful assessment to recognise the nature of the difficulty experienced by a child in understanding that the 9 in the number 937 (in the hundred position) represents 900. Assessing conceptual understanding needs closer observation and a good deal of probing. The role of probing questions in assessment is described, in more detail, later in this chapter.

Assessing problem-solving strategies

To become a good mathematician one needs to be an efficient problem solver and be able to undertake investigations with confidence. Development of mathematical processes such as making decisions, reasoning, working systematically, communicating ideas and generalising, which are part of 'Using and Applying Mathematics' in the National Curriculum (DfEE/QCA 1999), must form an integral part of mathematics teaching. The National Curriculum states that children are expected to try different approaches to problem solving, organise and check their results, discuss their mathematical work and explain their thinking. Assessing a child's competence in problem-solving strategies is more challenging as the skills needed are not easily measurable. Assessment of problem-solving skills will involve setting up of contexts and situations in which the use of these processes can be observed. This may be time-consuming, but worthwhile. Getting children to record their thoughts and methods in mathematical journals or diaries is one effective method of gathering evidence. Observing individual or group problem-solving activities and encouraging children to share their strategies with other children will also provide the teacher with opportunities for assessing this aspect of learning.

Assessing positive attitudes

Attitudes towards mathematics, such as confidence to tackle work, motivation, enjoyment and persistence, are important ingredients in the effective learning of mathematics. It is often tempting, in the midst of competing priorities in the classroom to overlook the assessment of this aspect. However, the assessment of attitudes does not have to be separately organised. Observation of children carrying out their mathematical tasks, the unsolicited comments they make during the introduction or conclusion of an activity and their recordings can often provide valuable information about attitudes. Occasionally, however, asking children to record their views on a completed task and their perceptions of what and how they are learning can be extremely helpful in judging their level of motivation, especially in light of many adults turning off the subject or even hating it later in life.

Types of assessment

The process of assessment is strongly linked to aspects of teaching and learning. The planning–learning/teaching–assessing cycle (Mitchell and Koshy 1995) shows that it is an ongoing dynamic with no specific starting point; they are interlinked (Figure 8.2). For assessment to be effective, it must become an integral part of the planning–learning/teaching–assessing cycle.

How does the cycle work in practice in the classroom? What are the implications? How can we ensure that our organisation of the planning and teaching stages contributes to effective mathematics learning? When considering classroom assessment, it is useful to explore the main types of assessment: day-to-day (short-term) formative and end of key stages (long-term) summative assessment. In the UK National Strategies for teaching mathematics, there is also reference to medium-term assessment.

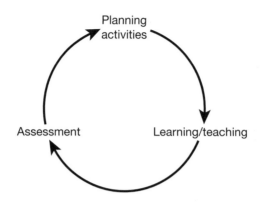

FIGURE 8.2 The planning–learning/teaching–assessing cycle (adapted from Mitchell and Koshy 1995).

During our visits to schools and working with teachers at the university, we have had many conversations with teachers about the crucial role of the planning–teaching–assessment cycle. Although school policies differ in the use of terminology, practice in most cases is based on the use of day-to-day assessment to inform future planning and end of block/term/half-term assessment to judge what children can do independently. In schools in England the Assessment of Pupils' Progress (APP) system (DCSF 2009) is used widely. Examples of an assessment policy and practice within a school are presented later in this chapter.

Short-term, formative assessment

The purpose of formative assessment is to provide ongoing information on children's learning, enabling teachers to identify their strengths and any aspects of their learning requiring attention. Assessment for learning involves formative assessment as the information collected helps the teacher when planning the next step in a child's learning or in deciding what action needs to be taken. In this dynamic process the teacher can give timely, useful feedback to the children and help them to set and monitor meaningful targets. The evidence gathered during formative assessment will also help the teacher to match learning material to the potential of the children and plan either remedial action or extension activities as required. We assess children's day-to-day learning in the following ways:

- *By listening to what children say.* This may be during their individual conversations with the teacher, in group and class discussions. It may be informal or through structured interviews or be focused on particular instances through targeted questioning.

- *By observing what children do.* This may be in the context of children counting a set of objects or performing an algorithm and selecting the steps within a calculation, or it may be based on the decisions they make and the nature of the processes they use when solving a mathematical problem or carrying out an extended investigation. Through observation a teacher can pick up much useful information about children's knowledge, skills and gaps in their understanding of concepts. Valuable information about children's attitudes towards different tasks and towards the subject of mathematics itself can also be gathered during classroom observations.

- *By analysing written work.* This may happen when the teacher is marking the work or sharing work with individual children. What children record on paper can provide significant insights into the strategies and procedures they use for calculations. Spending two or three minutes with children who have made mistakes provides the teacher with some understanding of their way of thinking and helps the teacher judge whether they hold any misconceptions.

All the ways of assessing described above help the teacher to build up an effective formative system that is an ongoing, day-to-day collection of information. This is different from the summative assessment carried out at the end of a term, end of a year or end of a key stage.

Through the short-term, day-to-day assessment the teacher can make sure that the main objectives of a lesson are learnt and understood, for example children know how to calculate effectively and the interconnected nature of fractions and decimals. If any difficulties in learning are highlighted, action can be taken through the next stage of planning. It is important that the learning objectives are shared with the children so that they can reflect on their learning and, through that reflection, let the teacher know of any difficulties and misconceptions. There are many ways to carry out day-to-day assessment. The teacher may work with particular groups in turn and focus on particular children on different days. Assessment can also be carried out at the time of marking work in the classroom or as part of homework or informal conversations. No specific recording may take place except informal jottings that can later be transferred into formal records. One of the other benefits of the day-to-day assessment is the opportunity it offers teachers or other adults in the classroom to review and reflect on their teaching methods and strategies and make adjustments if necessary.

Medium-term assessments (also known as periodic assessments) can be considered as formative in that they allow the teacher to assess the progress of the children over a period of time. It is more practical to assess what key objectives have been learnt in a term, what they can do and where there may be gaps. Also, during medium-term assessment, whether children have achieved their targets can be reviewed and new targets can be set. Records completed over a period can be more comprehensive and useful to highlight any gaps in children's learning, difficulties and patterns of mistakes and misconceptions.

Long-term, summative assessment

Summative assessment can take the form of national tests at the end of the year or end of Key Stages. Sometimes children carry out assessment tasks that provide overall evidence of their learning at a particular time. Information gathered from summative assessment is often used for the purpose of comparisons. League tables are constructed from the results of summative tests. Results from summative tests are also often used for evaluative purposes: to evaluate teaching methods and any general trends in children's achievement so that professional development and resources can be directed appropriately. One recent example comes to mind. In a local school it was found that in some end-of-year tests boys outperformed girls in mathematics. Short-term assessment had not highlighted any gender differences in attitudes or mathematical understanding of these children. The school set up an action research project to explore the reasons for this. As part of the project separate lessons were offered to boys and girls for part of the week and close observations were carried out in order to develop strategies to rectify the situation. Refined teaching strategies may also be considered to help improve children's performance. The results of the summative assessment are often reported to parents and sent to the next teachers or schools at the time of transfer. Clearly, effective short-term assessment can lead to effective long-term assessment as necessary action would have been taken if problems occurred.

Although summative assessment is a necessary part of teaching and learning, we need to be cautious about excessive emphasis on this kind of assessment. A systematic review by the EPPI Centre (2009) found that summative testing has a predominantly negative impact on students' motivation and that lower attaining students' learning was adversely affected by this form of assessment. The report included other negative influences of summative assessment, such as the anxiety it caused in students, especially girls, teachers adopting a transmission model of teaching, which disadvantaged students who preferred active approaches, and the tendency of teachers to adopt a narrower curriculum.

Benefits of day-to-day, formative assessment

Although good formative assessment will inevitably improve the outcomes of summative assessment, our emphasis in this chapter is to consider ways in which teachers can enhance their skills in formative assessment. Our decision to focus on formative assessment is based on our own belief that it is the day-to-day judgements on children's learning and how we respond to them that can make a real difference. Before drawing on research evidence about how formative assessment can help to raise achievement, we will try to make the distinction between the roles of summative and formative assessment clear by using an analogy. Think about a parent or carer. From a very early age a child is taken to a health clinic and, if necessary, to a doctor where he or she is measured using all sorts of criteria in order to assess whether his or her physical and mental development is within the normal range. If this is not the case then action is taken. This is done at different stages in a child's life and is a necessary process, but this alone will not help the child to develop. This is similar to the role of summative assessment: it is useful and necessary but not enough. Parents and carers also watch their children every day, feed them, keep them warm and comfortable and take note of their ups and downs, anxieties and worries as and when they manifest themselves. It is this everyday, ongoing care that helps the children feel secure and confident and plays a vital role in their growth and development. This ongoing care is similar to the role of formative assessment, which enables a teacher to act before it is too late to help to enhance their children's mathematical development and achievement.

The role of formative assessment in raising achievement

There is strong support from research for formative assessment. Based on an extensive survey of research findings, Black and Wiliam (1999) list the following five key factors (described by them as 'deceptively simple') that improve learning through assessment:

- the provision of effective feedback to pupils;
- the active involvement of pupils in their own learning
- adjusting teaching to take account of the results of assessment;
- a recognition of the profound influence assessment has on the motivation and self-esteem of pupils, both of which are crucial influences on learning;
- the need for pupils to be able assess themselves and understand how to improve. (p. 4)

In the context of assessment of learning, they also summarise the characteristics that promote learning. These are applicable to all learning, but are particularly relevant in the light of the contents of this chapter, which focuses on the role of assessment, leading to the effective learning of mathematics. The following conditions enhance learning opportunities:

- sharing learning goals with pupils;
- helping pupils to know and to recognise the standard they are aiming for;
- involving pupils in self-assessment;
- providing feedback, which leads to pupils recognising their next steps and how to take them. (p. 7)

Research points to the following as factors that inhibit student progress:

- a tendency for teachers to assess the quantity of work and presentation rather than the quality of learning;
- greater attention given to marking and grading, much of it tending to lower the self-esteem of pupils, rather than to providing advice for improvement;
- a strong emphasis on comparing pupils with each other, which demoralises the less successful learners.

We feel it is appropriate to conclude this section by drawing attention to what is considered important in teachers' assessment of pupils' work by the UK school inspectors (Ofsted 2000). They maintain that teachers' assessment of their pupils should focus on how well they look for gains in learning, gaps in knowledge and areas of misunderstanding, through their day-to-day work with pupils. This will include marking, questioning individuals and plenary sessions. Clues to the effectiveness of formative assessment are how well the teachers listen and respond to pupils, encourage and, where appropriate, praise them, recognise and handle misconceptions, build on their responses and steer them towards clearer understandings. They go on to say that effective teachers encourage pupils to judge the success of their own work and set targets for improvement and that they should take full account of the targets set out in individual plans for pupils with special educational needs.

Enhancing the quality of assessment in the classroom

In our dialogues with practising teachers we have come across many tick lists of children's acquisition of knowledge and skills that are listed in the National Curriculum. In many cases we could see very few pieces of work that demonstrated mathematical thinking, originality and elegance. We need to remind ourselves of the importance of mathematics, as is powerfully articulated in the introduction to the Mathematics National Curriculum (DfEE/QCA 1999: 60):

> Mathematics equips pupils with a uniquely powerful set of tools to understand and change the world. These tools include logical reasoning, problem solving skills, and the ability to think in abstract ways . . . . Mathematics is a creative discipline. It can stimulate moments of pleasure and wonder when a pupil solves a problem for the first time, discovers a more elegant solution to that problem, or suddenly sees hidden connections.

How can we assess the quality of children's mathematical learning and draw evidence of depth, elegance and creativity? In the following section we discuss some strategies and action that enable a teacher to enhance the quality of mathematical assessment and associated learning.

Effective questioning and interactions

The nature of the questions that teachers ask is of fundamental importance. In an action research project that was carried out by a group of thirty teachers, two aspects were highlighted. In paired group observations they found that 82 per cent of the questions asked by teachers in mathematics lessons were either closed or of 'lower order' (Bloom 1956). What also surprised the practitioners was that they were asking more open-ended and 'higher order' questions in other subject areas – English lessons, for example. To further illustrate the point, most of the questions asked (see examples in Box 8.1) elicited either one-word responses or easy descriptions.

BOX 8.1 Closed or lower order questions

- What is 9 add 7?
- How many sides does a square have?
- Can you tell me what a square looks like?
- What is the total of all the interior angles of a pentagon?
- How many ways can you complete this pattern?

Clearly, some of the these questions require some degree of mathematical thinking, but those teachers who then tried to design more open-ended questions acknowledged that open-ended and higher order questions encourage responses and communications that are more useful for the purpose of assessing children's mathematical thinking, understanding and possible misconceptions. Additionally, such questions, they claimed, demonstrate the mathematical learning potential of the children and the need for planning activities so that they are cognitively challenged. Examples of the newly designed questions are shown in Box 8.2.

BOX 8.2 Open-ended or higher order questions

- What is the same about these shapes? What is different?
- Which is the 'odd one' out in this list of numbers, shapes? Who agrees/disagrees with this?
- What would happen if I changed . . .?
- What have you discovered from this activity?
- What made you do it that way?
- How would you justify it, if I challenged your solution?

One of the teachers who trialled the new type of questions reported that not only did children give thirteen correct but different responses to the question 'Which is the odd one out of four shapes – a right-angled triangle, a rhombus, a square and a rectangle?', but also they gave explanations. This surprised her and also demonstrated how such questions were useful in assessing not only children's knowledge of vocabulary and properties of shape, but also the quality of children's mathematical thinking and reasoning.

Although closed questions have a role in learning, we do believe that for the purpose of assessment using open-ended questions can reveal a more in-depth and comprehensive profile of a child's mathematical understanding and potential.

The quality of our teaching is undoubtedly influenced by the type of questions we ask. As asking questions is an integral part of making assessments of children's learning, giving attention to the type of questions and how you ask them can often improve the quality of the information you collect. Concern for the quality of questions is raised by Black and Wiliam (1998), who reported that many research studies showed the dominance of 'recall' questions and that the use of higher order questions was infrequent.

The importance of interaction and the need to give children time to answer questions are highlighted in the Williams Report (2008). The review panel observed numerous examples of undue haste on the part of the practitioners during discussions with some children – in some cases even delivering the answers to their own questions before the child had time to formulate his or her own thoughts. Research by Siraj-Blatchford and Manni (2008) noted that 95 per cent of all the questions asked by early childhood staff were closed questions that required a recall of fact or a response from a limited selection of choices, and that only 5.5 per cent of questions were open-ended, which encourage children to speculate and offer potential for shared thinking/talking. Similar experiences found by our teacher-researchers were cited earlier.

Planning rich tasks for assessment

There is theoretical support for selecting rich tasks for the purpose of assessing children. Rich tasks would include opportunities for children to engage in higher order thinking and encourage them to discuss ideas with peers and adults. Vygotsky (1978) proposed that children can demonstrate and achieve higher levels of understanding if they are supported by a more knowledgeable adult or peer, through their zone of proximal development (ZPD). ZPD is the gap between what children can do unaided and what they can potentially do if supported. The implications of this theory are that we should use assessment tasks that are within the children's ZPD. Teachers need to know what children know (facts, skills) and can actually do, but they also need to provide opportunities for children to show their true potential by giving them tasks that are pitched just above their actual development, whether it be the next level in the National Curriculum or syllabus or an open-ended task which encourages them to use the kind of strategies that they are capable of.

Using a systematic sampling record for assessment

Although most of the assessment is carried out during the daily lesson, there are occasions when a systematic observation format, introduced by Mitchell and Koshy (1995), as can be seen in Figure 8.3, may be useful. The task description is given in Figure 8.4.

The formative assessment record reflects the true purpose of assessment and shows how the assessment cycle, planning–learning/teaching–assessing, actually works. The possible outcomes section lists the learning objectives of the activity. The teacher will observe what the child is doing and record in note form what the child does and says and the strategies used, and make a note of any other significant indicators such as boredom, anxiety, persistence and so on. The data collected are then transferred onto the record and studied by the teacher or by a group of teachers (for moderation) and interpretations made. Suggested action is also recorded. Action may vary according to the needs of the children. Linda, a class teacher, explained that action could involve extra support lessons, recommendation to attend master classes or a possible interview with the teacher or the mathematics coordinator to assess any aspects of the child's mathematics learning or attitudes that may need further exploration.

A systematic observation procedure may be used for diagnostic purposes or for assessing higher ability so that appropriate action for individual help and support can be arranged. In Linda's school the evidence collected during the sampling sessions is shared with the parents and is also used for target setting.

Providing feedback

An obvious point to make here is that the quality of feedback given to children is an important aspect of formative assessment. Because children's self-esteem plays an important role in maximising their achievement, this aspect needs very careful attention.

Formative Teacher Assessment Record

R ☐ Y1 ☐ Y2 ☐ Y3 ☑

Y4 ☐ Y5 ☐ Y6 ☐

Name: Anita Stainton .... Date: ....

Activity: GRAB ....

Possible Outcomes

- Counting (in groups ?) when handful is drawn, watch strategies
- Commutativity of multiplication and division.
- Times tables of × 2, × 3, × 4, × 5
- Idea of 'prime' numbers and vocabulary ?
- Addition of a string of numbers — strategies — mental?

Part (b) Discussion, working in a group, systematic work.

Account	Interpretation	Action
• Counted, in singles the first grab 24 and said :- 'you can share that into 2 and 3', then grouped into 4 and 5 to see if they work.	Not developed a good counting strategy — not attempted grouping.	Must show counting 'in groups' as more efficient to all children.
• Added scores accurately by writing as a 'sum'. Using fingers for bonds.	Commutativity Tables × 2 × 3, good recall — not × 4, × 5 Not yet fluent in calculations	Anika's target × 4 , × 5
• When 23 was obtained, said 'no, that will get no scores'	Awareness of 'Prime' numbers.	Use this context for a whole class discussion of 'Prime' numbers.
For Part (b) as with the other 2 in the group did not know where to start.	Lost!	The whole class— how to tackle investigation.

Comments: Part (b) was — if you could choose the
'best' number under 100, which one will
it be ?

FIGURE 8.3 A formative assessment sampling record (adapted from Mitchell and Koshy 1995).

Grab

A group activity – about 4 children

Materials: A pile of cubes or pebbles.

Players each grab a handful of cubes or pebbles.

The scoring system is as follows:
2 points if you can make sets of 2 with no remainder.
3 points if you can make sets of 3 with no remainder.
4 points if you can make sets of 4 with no remainder.
5 points if you can make sets of 5 with no remainder.

Thats the of the game – each player totals his points.

With 8 cubes the game would look like this.

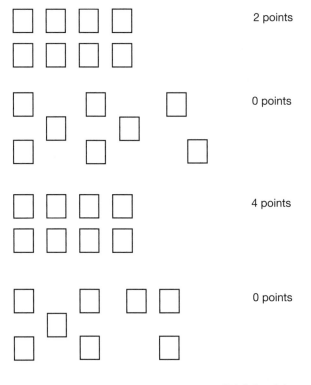

2 points

0 points

4 points

0 points

Total: 6 points

FIGURE 8.4 Task for close observation.

Marking children's work is one of the ways in which children receive feedback from adults. As the main purpose of marking is to assess children's progress and to plan action, it is worth reflecting on some principles that will enhance the quality of the marking process. First, when giving feedback, there may be a tendency for teachers to be guided by the quantity and presentation of work rather than focusing on the objectives of the lesson.

Butler (1988) compared the effects of giving marks as numerical scores, comments only and marks plus comments. Pupils given only comments made 30 per cent progress and all were motivated. No gains were made by those given marks plus comments. In both these groups the lower achievers also lost interest. The explanation was that giving marks cancelled out the beneficial effects of the comments. Careful commenting was found to work best when it stands on its own.

When marking children's work it is important to consider:

- that children should know what is expected of them;
- that if a child makes the same type of mistake on a whole page there is no need to mark them all with crosses;
- that asking children for explanations may be more helpful than crossing out work; a timely intervention may work better in improving the work;
- giving suggestions for improvement.

James *et al.* (2006) stress the importance of the teacher being aware of how effective feedback can help pupils to understand their strengths and weaknesses and improve their learning. Based on research findings the authors provide the following guidance for giving feedback to students:

- Feedback can be oral or written. There is no unequivocal evidence that one is better than the other – it depends on the context.
- Praise needs to be specific, describing what is praiseworthy, rather than generalised.
- Feedback is more effective if it focuses on the task (task involving) rather than the person (ego involving).
- Grades, marks, scores, ticks etc. have little effect on subsequent performance.
- Indicators of areas for improvement and possible strategies are better than total solutions (e.g. teachers' corrections of work) because pupils have to think. There are dangers in making public feedback that is related to individuals, but public feedback involving the whole class is valuable. Mistakes can be viewed as important learning opportunities.
- If pupils' efforts are recognised they are more likely to believe that they can improve. If they think success depends on innate ability they may give up in order to avoid failure.

Self-assessment and peer assessment by pupils

Research studies highlight the fact that self- and peer assessment enhance formative assessment, which in turn raises achievement. 'For formative assessment to be productive, pupils should be trained in self-assessment so that they can understand the main purpose of their learning and thereby grasp what they need to achieve' (Black and Wiliam 1998: 10). The authors maintain that the lack of this dimension of assessment being taken up is not because of the unreliability of children's assessment; in fact, children are generally 'honest and reliable in assessing themselves and one another and, if anything, can be too hard on themselves' (Black and Wiliam 1998: 10). The authors also suggest that the problem is mainly because pupils need to have a clear picture of which targets their learning is meant to attain. It is because of a passive learning mode that children find it difficult to assess their own learning. When we asked a group of teachers about their perceptions and practices about children's self-assessment, the majority of them admitted that they did not have a self-assessment system in operation, but the difficulty was explained in terms of lack of time. In the context of mathematics teaching and learning, if organised effectively there are two reasons for involving children in their own assessment. First, they will know what is expected of them as learners and, second, children will provide valuable insights into their own understanding through the process of assessing themselves. Black *et al.* (2003: 10) emphasise the need for children to have an understanding of what is expected of them for self-assessment to be effective: 'Pupils can only achieve a goal if they understand that goal and can assess what they need to do to achieve it'.

There is support for self-assessment and peer assessment from research. James *et al.* (2006) cite a study by Fontana and Fernandes (1994) in which, over a period of twenty weeks, primary school pupils were trained to carry out self-assessment. Over the period of the experiment the learning gains of this group were twice as big as those of a matching 'control' group. Black and colleagues (2003) found peer group assessment to be an important complement to self-assessment because pupils learn to take on the role of teachers and see learning from their perspective. At the same time they were able to give criticism and advice in a non-threatening way and in a language that children naturally use.

When children do not understand the intended learning outcomes they find it difficult to move beyond superficial criteria. By using a range of strategies and by dedicating time to allow children to reflect on and discuss their learning, teachers can develop children's peer assessment and self-assessment skills. It is recommended that the process of developing peer assessment and self-assessment skills be tackled in stages.

Children need to have the process modelled for them, using examples of work that demonstrate the intended learning outcomes, whether from previous teaching or examples from other children's work. Although children will need training in these aspects, the impact it has on learning will justify the effort. It is not essential for a complicated system to be in place from the outset. There are different levels of self-assessment that children can employ. Checklists and smiley faces can be a start. These can then be developed into a more detailed and structured format. We have found the introduction of mathematics journals helps children to become more reflective in the evaluation of their own work.

According to the UK Department for Education National Strategies children are not necessarily naturally self-evaluative so teachers need to invest time and commitment in developing strategies and opportunities that enable children to reflect upon their work and discuss their learning, thus promoting their development as independent learners and the ability to take responsibility for their own improvement and performance. This may be as part of the start of the lesson, which has a focus on sharpening mental maths skills and discussing strategies, as part of a mini-plenary within the main activity or at the end of a lesson.

Peer assessment

Peer assessment offers children rich opportunities to learn from each other, through speaking and listening, providing valuable feedback and even challenging each other to move beyond what they might have achieved on their own – thus perhaps aiding self-assessment in the future. Although perhaps more often used at Key Stage 2 (7- to 11-year-olds), we have observed peer assessment used at Key Stage 1 (4- to 6-year-olds), particularly during problem-solving activities, in which pupils are asked to reflect on each other's strengths and areas for development in mathematics, as well as how they have worked as a pair.

'Post-its' that 'stick on' are not only used as a means of teacher assessment but also can be an effective means of evaluating learning – in groups, pairs or individuals. These provide a quick way of encouraging pupils to think about their learning as well as next steps and provide teachers with a record of formative assessment from which future lessons can be planned and adapted.

'Talk partners' can also be used as a means of offering opportunities for children to develop questioning skills, which may be used to discuss and reflect upon each other's and their own work and to assess and offer feedback linked to learning objectives and success criteria. One of us recently overheard two pupils discussing the solution to a problem that involved the calculation 8×12:

Child A: 'Ok, so double 12 is 24, double 24 is 48 . . . .'

Child B: 'That's easy it's 96!'

Child A: 'Hang on, double 48 is 96, that's 8 times 12, yes it's 96.'

Child B: 'But my way was quicker.'

Child A: 'Yes, but how did you do it?'

Child B: 'I just knew my 12 times table! – actually I knew that $10 \times 8 = 80$ and that $80 + (2 \times 8)$, 16, is 96.'

Child A: 'Oh, I just used doubles but that's ok isn't it?'

Child B: 'Well we both got to the answer but I suppose it's good to know your times tables 'cos it's quicker – put 12 times on your target card.'

Following this observation the class teacher used the plenary session to recap on the learning that had taken place and these two children volunteered their assessments of each other and articulated where they thought they were at in their mathematical understanding. Both the children felt that they understood how to tackle the problem but agreed that one had a more efficient method upon which the other child identified a personal target.

Using student mathematical reflective journals

An effective way of assessing and recording work, which can encourage self-assessment and peer assessment (if it is shared with peers), is by introducing student mathematical journals. These can help to demonstrate the child's level of understanding or misconceptions, use of vocabulary and the nature of the strategies used. A journal can also be used as a discussion document between the teacher and child.

Figure 8.5 shows a sample grid that can be used for facilitating children to reflect on their work, at the end of a session or as part of homework. It is intended to be used not at the end of each session, but periodically and with a range of different activities to sample the level of children's thinking and understanding. It is important to design a format that gives children a sufficient amount of space to record their thoughts. It is useful to remember that it takes time for children to think and write reflectively if they are not used to it. During a university intervention programme when we trialled the use of these journals, children recorded just one phrase or short sentence in the

---

Name.............................

Date...............................

1. What was the lesson about?

2. What did you do?

3. This is what I learnt

4. This is the maths I used

5. It was easy/quite hard/very hard. *(underline 'one' of these and explain your reason)*

6. Did this work connect with anything you have learnt before?

7. Do you see anything here you use in everyday life?

8. Is there anything you are not sure about?

9. What would you like to find out more about?

FIGURE 8.5 Student's mathematical journal.

boxes at the beginning. In time, the detail and the amount and the quality of the recording improved significantly.

Construction of concept maps and glossaries

How well a concept is understood can be assessed by asking pupils to construct concept maps of ideas. A good concept map will show how a child understands an idea and how that idea is connected to other ideas. For example, a map of decimals may show connecting links to fractions and percentages. It may also show how decimals fit into the base ten numeration system. A multiplication concept map may show its connections to addition and division. We have used concept maps with our teacher training students and found that they can help to assess the level of understanding, as well as any misconceptions and gaps. From a constructivist view of learning, which places children at the centre of learning as constructors of their own knowledge, it can be assumed that the more connections are made, the deeper a person's understanding of a concept.

Target setting

Target setting happens at different levels. Here we are focusing on setting targets for individual children. Target setting should follow many of the assessment procedures described in this chapter. Test results, day-to-day observation and listening, systematic sampling of children's work, self-assessment and portfolios can all be taken into account for target setting purposes. In the context of this chapter, the following general principles of target setting are worthy of consideration. Targets:

- should be set based on clearly explained learning objectives;
- should be related to assessment data;
- should be set in partnership with the child;
- should be expressed in a language that children can understand;
- should be realistic and manageable;
- should set a 'just enough' challenge for the child;
- should explain what indicators of success are;
- should be monitored and revised regularly.

Use of portfolios

Encouraging children to keep a portfolio of their best work is a step towards more effective self-assessment. Black and Wiliam (1998) define a portfolio as a collection of a student's work usually constructed by selecting from a larger corpus and often presented with a reflective piece written by the student justifying the selection.

Involving children in selecting their best pieces of work by judging against a list of criteria – these could include depth of understanding, level of competency, use of mathematical processes, elegance and fluency – would enable them to reflect on their own work and set their own targets. Mitchell and Koshy (1995) found that children took great pride in collecting pieces of work for their portfolios. However, it needed a great deal of effort on the part of the teachers to train children to evaluate their work before selecting their best efforts. At their best, portfolios can provide the following benefits to children's learning and assessment:

- They increase the motivation to learn.
- They give children some ownership of their own learning.
- They celebrate children's achievement – with some training, children will learn to be self-critical and reflect on their own learning.
- Children will strive to do better than their previous attempt rather than compete with peers.
- They provide a basis for homework and parents' evening discussions.
- The intrinsic satisfaction of constructing a record of achievement acts as a valuable reward and helps to develop self-esteem.

As a portfolio of work provides a systematic collection of work, it can provide valuable information about all elements of learning: knowledge, skills, effort, achievement, quality of thinking, students' needs, progress and task commitment. If worked in partnership with the teacher, it can become a tool for reflection and demonstrate students' special strengths, misunderstandings and special needs.

A portfolio allows the teacher to gain insights into the nature of children's thinking and connectedness between ideas. It is useful for showcasing children's work for different purposes.

From principle to practice

In this section we present some models of assessment that are being developed by Cherry Blossom Primary School (300 children, aged 5 to 11) with the aim of gathering a comprehensive profile of children as developing mathematicians. The staff at Cherry Blossom hope not only that this will benefit their understanding of children's progress linked to the level descriptors in the National Curriculum, but also that the strategies used will be effective in personalising the learning opportunities for individuals, as well as promoting enjoyment and engagement in mathematics within the school.

The introduction of the Assessment of Pupils' Progress (APP) (DCSF 2009) from the National Strategies has provided teachers with a useful tool for assessing pupil progress. However, teachers at Cherry Blossom felt that this paints only part of the picture so they have developed what they call 'layers' of assessment to help build a more complete picture. These 'layers' are:

- day-to-day assessment;
- end of block/half-term/term assessment;
- peer and self-assessment development;
- use of structured portfolios.

We will now address each of these in more detail.

Day-to-day assessment

This is also known as 'assessment for learning' and is used by teachers to gather information about children's developing knowledge of mathematical facts, skills and conceptual understanding, which will enable them to move on to the next step. It is also an opportunity to discover any misconceptions and address them immediately – perhaps using them as a teaching point for the whole class. How is this information gathered and recorded? At Cherry Blossom school it begins at the planning stage, during which teachers and teaching assistants work closely together to consider how the key learning objectives will be met through the planned activities. They then consider key questions, mathematical vocabulary and what to look for when assessing groups and individuals. A 'sticky label system' is used by both the class teacher and the teaching assistant to quickly record observations, conversations and whiteboard jottings during carpet time and these are attached to the pupils' individual mathematics record card or onto the planning sheet – often a weekly plan, but here it is shown as an individual lesson plan (see Figure 8.6).

'Guided group work' as advocated in the Williams Review (2008) plays a key role in gathering rich data on pupils' understanding through observation, speaking and listening. Teaching assistants are trained to carry out observations and a focus group

---

🌸 Cherry Blossom Primary

Year 3   Maths: Identifying properties of shapes/lines of symmetry — No. in group 30

Specific learning needs	Previous learning/experience to be built upon:	Resources
Jason-sits near the front of the class to aid his hearing-- may need support to work in groups. Muna may need support as she lacks confidence in maths. She may find physical resources useful as a prompt. Cathryn-very able-demonstrates secure knowledge of names of shapes but do check understanding	Rose, Willow and Honeysuckle groups can use mathematical names for common 2-D shapes. Sort shapes and describe some of their features, e.g. number of sides, corners, edges, faces. Sycamore & hollyhocks still need work on names & properties for some 2-D but do recognise circle, square and triangle & properties	Large 2-D shape cards (include irregular shapes) Set of small 2-D shape cards per pair Large mirror Large paper oblong, e.g. A4 sheet **Vocabulary**: Previously taught: circle, triangle, square, rectangle, pentagon, hexagon, octogaon, sides, corners, right angle, reflection, symmetrical, mirror line, line of symetry New: vertex, vertices

NC. Ma3 2b visualise and describe 2-D and 3-D shapes and the way they behave, making more precise use of geometrical language, especially that of triangles, quadrilaterals, and prisms and pyramids of various kinds; recognise when shapes are identical.
2c make and draw with increasing accuracy 2-D and 3-D shapes and patterns; recognise reflective symmetry in regular polygons; recognise their geometrical features and properties including angles, faces, pairs of parallel lines and symmetry, and use these to classify shapes and solve problems.

Learning objectives	Activities (inc. differentiation and us of ICT, key, vocab, questions)	Assessment
To identify properties of 2-D shapes Cathryn shows understanding of properties of shapes as well as names	Play the game same or different Show on of the large 2-D shape cards. Children choose on of the cards from their selection that is the same in one/some way. Q. How is you shape the same as mine? Repeat several times. Encourage pupils to consider: • number of sides • number of verticals • whether sides are the same length • whether or not angles are right angles. Invite another child to select a shape that is different in one/some way. Q. How is your shape different from mine? *Faizah recognised right-angles in a rectangle*	**What**: ability to identify what is the same and what is different using correct vocabulary **How**: Use TA to note those struggling. Who: focus on Jenna and Muna + hollyhock group **Assessment**

FIGURE 8.6 Lesson plan.

feedback sheet is used to document the learning that has taken place, as shown in Figure 8.7. In addition, teacher observations, photos of evidence and recording what the children say on the Easy Speak Microphones are all used as a means of day-to-day assessment with individual targets displayed on a wall chart for children to refer to. At Cherry Blossom, although detailed planning is important, openness and flexibility are encouraged so that teachers can easily amend input and activities without feeling that they have to spend hours completely rewriting a lesson.

End of block, end of half-term or end of term assessment

These may be carried out using a given task to assess what the children can do individually and to assess strengths and difficulties within a block of work or at a key point within the school year. These assessments are more closely linked to 'levels' and outcomes are recorded on a grid using a traffic light system (red = not yet met; amber = working towards; green = secure understanding, as shown in Figure 8.8). Here the APP format is used on six children across the ability range for benchmarking within the class and the year group.

Developing peer and self-assessment

Until now, peer and self-assessment have often been used only in literacy lessons at Cherry Blossom Primary, but they are currently trialling models that adopt a smiley face system for self-assessment for use in the mathematics lessons – particularly for the 5- to 7-year-olds. You will see from the example given in Figure 8.9 that there is a focus on collaborative working as well as understanding of the key learning objectives. Peer assessment is being piloted for those between 7 and 11 years with opportunities for talk partners to consider some key questions about each other's learning, as seen in Figure 8.10.

Structured portfolios

Work is, at present, recorded in books and on worksheets, but with an emphasis on speaking and listening and planned guided group work within the mathematics lessons. Children have richer opportunities to share ideas, develop vocabulary and focus on applications of facts and skills in developing an understanding of key concepts through problem-solving tasks. A structured portfolio has been developed for each child, which includes samples of work, jottings, snapshot recordings of learning episodes and photographs, as well as the peer and self-assessment records. A list of targets and children's responses to their targets are also included. This is proving really useful as a means of building up a holistic view of individuals and emerging young mathematicians. Children have been keen to take an active role in their learning and in the submission of evidence to their portfolios. The portfolios have, so far, proved useful for parents to have a real sense of their child's strengths and areas for development – not only in mathematical knowledge and understanding, but also in the way they engage with learning.

				Cherry Blossom Primary	

Cherry Blossom Primary

Focus Activity Feedback Sheet

Date: 3/11/09   Class: 3

Learning objectives:
To identify properties of 2-D shapes
To identify symmetry in 2-D shapes

Outline of activity
Children work in groups of six to investigate lines of symmetry in 2-D shapes. Children record their findings.

Key vocabulary/questions: sides, corners, right angle, reflection, symmetrical, mirror line, line of symmetry. New: vertex, vertices
Q. How can we find if a shape in symmetrical?
Q. Is this shape symmetrical? Without using a mirror how can you show that it is? (Think pair square)
Q. Would anyone have done it differently?
Q. Are there any other ways in which you could fold the shape so that both sides of the fold are equal?
Q. How many lines of symmetry does this shape have?

Resources: Large 2-D shaped cards (including irregular shapes), set of small 2-D shape cards per pair group, large mirror, large paper oblong.

Name	☺	☺	☹	Comments	Next steps (completed by teacher)
Sophie		✓		Able to identify line of symmetry for regular triangle, pentagon and hexagon by folding, more challenging when more than one line of symmetry.	More on identifying more than one line of symmetry, sorting and classifying accordingly.
Abdul	✓			Able to identify line of symmetry for regular triangle, pentagon and hexagon by folding, used mirror to check. Recognised that irregular shapes do not have line of symmetry.	Sketch reflection of simple shape in mirror line parallel to one edge where edges parallel or perpendicular.
Janack	✓			Was able to identify line of symmetry for regular triangle, pentagon and hexagon by folding, used mirror to check. Systematic in recording findings.	Sketch reflection of simple shape in mirror line parallel to one edge where edges parallel or perpendicular.
Kyle		✓		Able to identify line of symmetry for regular triangle, pentagon and hexagon by folding, more challenging when more than one line of symmetry.	Identifying more than one line of symmetry, sorting and classifying accordingly.
Jasmine			✓	Really struggled with concept of symmetry, especially those with more than one line.	Need to revisit making symmetrical pattern using peg board.
Anna	✓			Was able to identify line of symmetry for all shapes used by folding, used mirror to check. Systemetrical in recording findings, able to classify according to lines of symmetry.	Sketch reflection of simple shape in mirror line parallel to one edge where edges parallel or perpendicular.
Bela		✓		Able to identify line of symmetry for regular triangle, pentagon and hexagon by folding, more challenging when more than one line of symmetry.	Identifying more than one line of symmetry, sorting and classifying accordingly.

FIGURE 8.7 Focus activity feedback sheet.

Cherry Blossom Primary

Pupil Progress Record
Key learning objectives are in bold
Normally traffic light colours are used to indicate levels of progress but here we use variations in text to show this with colours that would be used in brackets
Key to progress: not yet achieved – underlined (red); working towards – normal text (yellow); secure understanding – italics (green)

Name: Hayley Smith   **Year 3**

Level	Numbers and the numbers system	Calculations	Solving problems	Holding data	Shape and space	Measures
3c	*Know what each digit in a 3 digit number represents* **Order numbers to 100** Multiply integers by 10 **Count on or back in tens or hundreds from any 2 or 3 digit number** **Recognise unit fractions of whole numbers and shapes** **Begin to recognise** simple equivalent fractions, **understand and use £. p. notation**	*Know by heart all +/– facts for each number to 20* Add or subtract mentally a near multiple of 10 to/from a 2 digit number **Bridge through a multiple of 10 and then adjust** *Recognise + as inverse of multiplication* *Begin to find remainders after division* Use known facts and place value to carry out mentally simple ×/÷, Check with an equivalent calculation *Know by heart facts from the 2, 5, and 10 multiplication tables*	Solve word problems using one or more steps **Explain how problem was solved** orally and where appropriate in writing Use mental addition and subtraction simple multiplication & division to solve simple word-problems	*Construct and begin to interpret bar graphs and pictograms labeled in ones then twos* Organise numerical data into Venn and Carroll diagrams (2 criteria)	**Identify and draw lines of symmetry and recognise shape with no lines of symmetry** *Identify and compare right angles with other angles* Plot points on a grid	Known relationship between familiar measures Read labelled and unlabelled scale **Use and know relationship between units of time**

FIGURE 8.8 Pupil progress record.

 **Cherry Blossom Primary Self-Assessment**

Name: ....   **Date** ....

How well did I listen to other people's ideas?

How well did I share my own ideas?

How well did my partner and I discuss strategies and come to a decision?

How well was I able to identify 2-D shapes according to their properties?

How well was I able to identify lines of symmetry in 2-D shapes?

FIGURE 8.9 Cherry Blossom Primary self-assessment.

 **Cherry Blossom Primary Peer Assessment**

- Find one example of a shape with one or more lines of symmetry you are really proud to have discovered and circle it. Tell the person next to you why you are pleased with it.

- Decide with your talk partner which of the success criteria you have been most successful with and which one needs help or could be taken even further.

- (After whole-class sharing for a minute or two). You have three minutes to identify shapes according to their properties and then take it in turns to tell your partner – how well did each of you do?

- You have five minutes to find *one* aspect of properties of shape where you could improve. Write your improvement at the bottom of you work.

- Look back at the problems you have solved today. Where were you successful? What approach did you take?

FIGURE 8.10 Cherry Blossom Primary peer assessment.

Summary

In this chapter we have attempted to discuss aspects of assessing mathematical learning. In considering the purposes of assessment, our main emphasis was on the role of formative assessment, which was considered against the background of the principles within the distinct Assessment for Learning. Drawing on research and personal experiences, we discussed ways of enhancing the quality of classroom assessment by suggesting practical strategies. We also addressed issues relating to feedback and self- and peer assessment, and the innovative uses of student reflective journals and portfolios. Classroom examples are provided at the end of the chapter to exemplify the principles discussed.

References

Askew, M., Rhodes, V., Brown, M., Wiliam, D. and Johnson, D. (1997) *Raising Attainment in Numeracy.* Report of a project funded by the Nuffield Foundation. London: King's College.

Assessment Reform Group (2002) *Assessment for Learning: Beyond the Black Box.* Cambridge: School of Education, Cambridge University.

Black, P. and Wiliam, D. (1998) *Inside the Black Box: Raising Achievement through Classroom Assessment.* London: King's College.

Black, P. and Wiliam, D. (1999) *Assessement for Learning: Beyond the Black Box.* Cambridge: School of Education, Cambridge University.

Black, P., Harrison, C., Marshall, B. and William, D. (2003) *Assessment for Learning: Putting It into Practice.* Maidenhead: Open University Press.

Bloom, B. S. (1956) *Taxonomy of Educational Objectives,* Volume 1. Harlow: Longman.

Butler, R. (1988) 'Enhancing and undermining intrinsic motivation: the effects of task-involving and ego-involving evaluation on interest and performance', *British Journal of Educational Psychology,* 58: 1–14.

Cockcroft, W. H. (1982) *Mathematics Counts: Report of the Committee of Inquiry into the Teaching of Mathematics in Schools.* London: HMSO.

DCSF (Department for Children, Schools and Families) (2009) *Guidance for School Improvement Partners: Supporting and Challenging Improvement in AfL with APP.* London: DCSF.

DfEE/QCA (Department for Education and Employment/Qualifications and Curriculum Authority) (1999) *The National Curriculum: A Handbook for Primary Teachers in England.* London: DfEE.

EPPI Centre (2009) *A Systematic Review of the Impact of Summative Assessment and Tests on Students' Motivation for Learning.* London: EPPI Centre. Available at http://www.ttrb.ac.uk.

Ernest, P. (2000) 'Teaching and learning mathematics', in Koshy, V., Ernest, P. and Casey, R. (eds) *Mathematics for Primary Teachers.* London: Routledge.

Fontana, D. and Fernandez, M. (1994) 'Improvement in mathematics performance as a consequence of self-assessment in Portuguese primary school pupils', *British Journal of Educational Psychology,* 64: 407–417.

Her Majesty's Inspectorate (HMI) (1985) *Mathematics 5–16: Curriculum Matters.* London: HMSO.

James, M., Black, P., Carmichael, P., Conner, C., Dudley, P., Fox, A., Frost, D., Honour, L., MacBeath, J., McCormick, R., Marshall, B., Pedder, D., Procter, R., Swaffield, S. and Wiliam, D. (2006) *Learning How to Learn: Tools for Schools.* London: Routledge.

Koshy, V. (2000) 'Children's mistakes', in Koshy, V., Ernest, P. and Casey, R. (eds) *Mathematics for Primary Teachers.* London: Routledge.

Mitchell, C. and Koshy, V. (1995) *Teacher Assessment: Looking at Children's Learning.* London: Hodder and Stoughton.

Ofsted (2000) *Handbook for Inspecting Primary and Nursery Schools.* London: Office for Standards in Education.

Siraj-Blatchford, I. and Manni, L. (2008) 'Would you like to tidy up now? An analysis of adult questioning in the English Foundation Stage', *Early Years: An International Journal for Research and Development,* 28 (1): 5–22

Vygotsky, L. (1978) *Mind in Society.* Cambridge, MA: Harvard University Press.

Williams, P. (2008) *Independent Review of Mathematics Teaching in Early Years Setting and Primary Schools.* London: DCSF.

Index

acceleration 145
addition, strategies for 58–60
Ainley, J. 68
algorithms: algorithm clingers, low attainment
and 115–18; arithmetical algorithms 19; gifted
children and 132, 135; mental algorithms
19, 22; numeracy, aspects of 19, 22; for
subtraction 21, 27n16
Andrews, P. and Massey, H. 66
arithmetic: arithmetical algorithms 19; laws of
arithmetic 48; *see also* mental arithmetic
arithmogon 98, 105
art, mathematics in 34–6
articulation, mathematical vocabulary and 120–2
Askew, M. 28, 29, 91, 95
Askew, M. and Wiliam, D. 78, 84, 88–90
Askew, M. *et al.* 29, 50, 67, 153–4
Askew, M., Robinson, D. and Mosley, F. 58
assessment of learning 150–77; Assessment
Reform Group, principles of assessment
(2002) 151–3; attitudes, assessment of
positivity in 155; classroom assessment
150; closed questions 161; concept
maps, construction of 169; conceptual
understanding, assessment of 153–4; creativity
160; day-to-day assessment 156–7, 158–9,
171–2; definition of 150–2; end of block,
end of half-term or end of term assessment
172; facts, assessment of 152; feedback
provision 162–5, 173; feedback provision,
guidance on 167; formative assessment 156–7;
formative assessment, day-to-day, benefits of
158–9; formative assessment, role in raising
achievement 159–60; glossaries, construction
of 169; higher-order questions 161; inhibition
of student progress, factors affecting 159;
interactions, questioning and, effectiveness
in 160–2; learning through assessment,
key factors in 159; long-term, summative

assessment 157–8; lower-order questions 160;
marking work, feedback and 164–5; models
of assessment 170–6; objectives in teaching
maths 152; Ofsted perspective 159–60;
open-ended questions 161; peer assessment
167; peer assessment, development of 172;
periodic assessments 157; planning of rich
tasks for assessment 162, 164; portfolios, use
of 169–70; practical models of assessment
170–6; problem-solving strategies, assessment
of 155; process of 150–2; promotion of
learning, characteristics of 159; pupil
progress record, example of 174; quality
of assessment in classroom, enhancement
of 160–5; questioning and interactions,
effectiveness in 160–2; reflective journals, use
of 167–9; rich tasks for assessment, planning
of 162, 164; self-assessment 165–70, 175;
self-assessment, development of 172; self-
assessment, modelling of process for students
166; short-term, formative assessment 156–7;
skills, assessment of 153; structured portfolios
172; summative assessment 157–8; systematic
sampling record, use of 162, 163; 'talk
partners', peer assessment and 167; target
setting 169; testing at end of learning 150–2;
types of 155–6; Williams Report, perspective
on assessment 151
Assessment of Pupils' Progress (APP) 156, 170,
172
Assessment Reform Group 150–2; principles of
assessment (2002) 151–2
Association of Mathematics Teachers 42
assumption in problem-solving 98, 105, 108
attitudes: assessment of positivity in 155; to
mental calculation 45

bar charts 72
Bird, R. 114, 117, 118

179